How to G
Web Site

Books Available

Other Titles of Interest

BP404 How to Create Pages for the Web Using HTML

BP532 How to Use XML

BP539 Easy PC Web Site Construction

* * * * *

BP610 How to Make Your Own Web Site for the Older Generation

How to Get Your Web Site Noticed

by

Kevin Ryan

**Bernard Babani (Publishing) Ltd,
The Grampians,
Shepherds Bush Road,
London W6 7NF
England**

www.babanibooks.com

How to Get Your Web Site Noticed

Please Note

Although every care has been taken with the production of this book to ensure that any projects, designs, modifications and/or programs, etc., contained herewith, operate in a correct and safe manner and also that any components specified are normally available in Great Britain, the Publishers and Author(s) do not accept responsibility in any way for the failure (including fault in design) of any project, design, modification or program to work correctly or to cause damage to any equipment that it may be connected to or used in conjunction with, or in respect of any damage or injury that may be so caused, nor do the Publishers accept responsibility in any way for the failure to obtain specified components.

Notice is also given that if equipment that is still under warranty is modified in any way or used or connected with home-built equipment then the warranty may be void.

© 2006 Bernard Babani (publishing) Ltd.

First Published-August 2006

British Library Cataloguing in Publication Data:

A catalogue record for this book is available from the British Library

ISBN 0 85934 566 1

Cover Design by Gregor Arthur
Printed and Bound in Great Britain by Cox & Wyman Ltd., Reading.

About this Book

How to get Your Web Site noticed was written to help people, who are creating web sites for business or pleasure, to understand the key factors that determine how visible that web site will be on the internet. By visible, I mean how often the pages that make up that web site are returned in response to a search that contains keywords from the web site and how high up the results list a web page is placed.

Creating a web site is an exciting and challenging activity where you learn many new skills. You get great satisfaction seeing your completed web pages available to everybody on the internet. However, there is another stage to the process, which is getting the search engines to recognise that you have created a valuable addition to the totality of information available on the Internet.

The material in the book is written in a sequential way, meaning that you should work your way through it chapter by chapter. The information you need to know first appears first. There are exercises and checklists to help you understand the subject matter and create a programme of work to improve your web pages respectively.

This book was written with the assumption that the reader knows how to create a web site and how to move those web pages from a PC to a web server using FTP. Other than that, no prior computer or internet knowledge is required. It is hoped that by using its guidelines you will get a buzz from seeing your web pages appearing regularly in the search engines' results pages!

About the Author

Kevin Ryan graduated as a Telecommunications & Radio Engineer and spent the early part of his career with the BBC maintaining and developing radio monitoring equipment. After a period as a project engineer with the BBC World Service he returned to BBC Monitoring to lead the newly formed computer engineering team. This was his first experience of deploying a search engine or text retrieval system as it was then known. He spent the next 20 years researching, testing and deploying search engines both inside and outside the corporate network.

He currently runs his own company specialising in internet solutions for the small business sector.

Trademarks

All brands and product names used in the book are recognised as trademarks, or registered trademarks, of their respective companies.

Contents

1. Search Engine Overview 1
Before Google 1
Types of Search Engines.. 3
Search Engine League Tables 5
Direct Search Engines 7
Search Engine Relationships............................... 8
   Exercise 1 10
Directory Search Engines 11
Search or Directory... 13
Directory Relationships....................................... 15
Pay per Click 17
Specialist Search Engines 18
How Search Engines Index the Web 19
The Google Index 22
Ranking 23
Web Behaviour 23
Search Behaviour 24
Google PageRank 27
Checklist 1 30
   Exercise 2 31

2. Web Site Improvements................................. 33
Web Site Health Check....................................... 33
   Minimum Amount of Content......................... 34
   Robots & Humans 35
   Too Many Images 35
   Using Frames.. 37
   Dynamically Generated Web Pages 40

- Using Free Hosting Space 41
- Complicated Web Pages................................. 41
- URL with Special Characters 42
- Welcome Page.. 42
- Deep Pages 42
- Old Pages 42
- Flash Pages 43
- Hidden Text.. 43
- Hosting Problems... 43
- Valid HTML Code.. 44
- Redirection... 45
- Note on Checklists 46
- Checklist 2 47
- Create a High Ranking Web Site 48
- Crossing the Quality Threshold 50
- Step 1: Web Site Review 50
  - Step 1A - Web Site Architecture..................... 51
  - Step 1B - Web Site Theme 54
  - Exercise 3 54
  - Exercise 4 55
  - Checklist 3 57
- Practical Example... 59
  - Step 1C - Logical Structure 59
  - Step 1D - Keywords 62
  - Ideal Site Structure.. 65
  - Step 1E - Analysis... 67
  - Exercise 5 67
  - Step 1F - Learning Lessons 69
  - Checklist 4 71

- Step 2: Action Plan for Change 71
  - Step 2A - Keyword Research 74
  - Step 2B - Keyword Analysis 80
  - Step 2C - Keyword Refinement 82
  - Step 2D - Applying the Keyword Research 83
  - Exercise 6 85
  - Exercise 7 85
- Step 3 - Making the Changes 87
- Internal PageRank 88
  - Exercise 8 88
- Meta Tags 89
  - META HTTP TAGS 91
  - META NAME TAGS 92
  - Checklist 5 95

3. Search Engine Submission 97
- Manual URL Submission 97
  - Checklist 6 98
  - Google 99
  - MSN 106
  - Yahoo 109
  - Search Engine Directories 111
  - Does it Work? 116
  - Specialist Directory 118
  - DMOZ 119
  - Monitoring Progress 119

4. Advanced Techniques 121
- Checking the Indexes 121
  - Google Spider Emulator 124
  - Checklist 7 126

How to Get Your Web Site Noticed

- Accessing Your Server Logs 127
  - The Robots File... 130
  - Web Statistics 131
  - Search Phrases... 136
  - HTTP Error Codes 137
  - Actual Code Numbers 138
  - Cracking the Code 140
  - The Client Error Codes 141
- Google AdWords 144
  - Keyword Driven Campaign 146
  - Site Targeted Campaign 153
  - Google Network 155
  - Does it Work? 156
  - Checklist 8 157

5. Search Engine Optimization.......................... 159
- Applying Optimization 159
- General Optimization Advice 161
  - On The Page Factors.................................... 162
  - <HEAD> Region... 162
  - <TITLE> Tag... 162
  - META Description Tag 163
  - META Keyword Tag 163
- Keyword Metrics 163
  - Keyword frequency 164
  - Keyword Weight 164
  - Exercise 9 166
  - Keyword Prominence 166
  - Keyword Example 1 167
  - Keyword Example 2 168

xi

    \<BODY\> TAG 168
    Checklist 9 170
  Specific Optimization Advice 171
    MSN Optimization 172
    ASK Optimization 175
    Yahoo Optimization 177
    Google Optimization.................................... 177

6. Advanced Tools 180
  Browsers... 181
    Internet Explorer.. 181
    Firefox 181
    Opera 181
    Lynx 181
  Accessibility 182
  Free Tools 184
    Free Monitor for Google 184
    Hello Engines... 186
    Internet Business Promoter......................... 188
    Web CEO 193
    SEO Studio 196
    Accurate Monitor For Search Engines 199
    Google API... 200
    Yahoo API 200
    Just How Useful are the Tools? 202

7. Controlling the Robots 206
  robots.txt... 207
  META Tags... 209
    Where to put the Robots META tag 210
    What to put into the Robots META tag.......... 210

- Google Sitemaps 211
  - GSiteCrawler 214
  - Google Sitemaps Interface 219
- ALEXA Toolbar 222
- **Glossary** **226**
- **Appendix 1** **235**
- **Index** **240**

1. Search Engine Overview

Search engines have been around for some time now and are an essential part of the internet. Without them most of us would be unable to find the information, products or services that we are looking for. This book is about Internet search engines such as Google & MSN. It does not cover the other type of search engines such as Verity Search and RetrievalWare that are purchased by large corporate enterprises and deployed on Intranets or as specialist applications on internet sites. Companies like Google will provide a similar service to operate behind the firewalls of company networks but the two cousins co-exist quite happily in their separate domains. There are a lot of similarities between the two types and it is interesting to note that advancements in refining search results and in summarising a document to determine its theme that are now being considered by Google & Yahoo have been used for many years by big companies.

Before Google

If we ever need a search engine time frame it should probably be designated as BG (Before Google) and AG (After Google)! It is now hard to imagine but just a few years ago nobody had heard of Google or even the World Wide Web! As late as 1990 it just wasn't considered necessary to be able to search for documents on the Internet. The fledging Internet was used mainly as an information exchange tool between people who knew <u>exactly what</u> they were looking for and <u>where</u> to look for it.

1 Search Engine Overview

This is almost the converse of what a search engine is for – it finds information for people who just have an idea what they are looking for but don't know where it is located.

The concept and development of a search engine started as an academic exercise and many early tools appeared and just as quickly disappeared as various Universities had their students tackle this interesting problem. The 'web' was so small ten years ago that there was no commercial reason to invest in developing software that would try to find and catalogue every piece of information stored in cyberspace.

The first search engine that we would identify with was called the WebCrawler and was deployed in 1994. This was a major leap forward as the WebCrawler indexed whole pages rather than just the header information that is usually hidden by today's browsers. It only found a few hundred thousand pages but this was enough to encourage others to push forward with new ideas. Soon after that Lycos came on the scene and with its more advanced software it soon showed that the web was really a huge entity.

After 6 months Lycos had found nearly 70 million pages of information. Although nothing like the size of the Internet today this was a staggering revelation and people began to see the potential of presenting this disjointed information in a more coherent way. Within another three years all the now familiar names appeared on the search engine scene: Excite (1996); Overture (1997); AltaVista (1997); Ask Jeeves (1997); Google (1998) and MSN (1998). A whole new industry had been born and like all industries it would be subject to mergers and acquisitions that have now created essentially four big players and a host of minor and niche search engines.

Search Engine Overview 1

This is a rapidly developing and competitive industry as just getting a small fraction of the huge number of searches that are carried out each day can be lucrative. It is important to keep abreast of developments and you should subscribe to one or two of the more expert newsletters on the topic.

Types of Search Engines

Type	Used For	Examples
Primary Search Engine	Searching for documents or web pages using keywords as the input.	Google, Yahoo MSN, Ask
Directory Search Engines	Another form of direct search. Searching for web sites sorted by category.	DMOZ, Yahoo Linkopedia, Mirago
Meta Search Engine	To search across several search engines at the same time.	Dogpile, Hotbot, MetaCrawler
Pay per Click	To supplement primary search engines by offering paid listings that are charged on a usage basis.	Google Adwords, Yahoo

Fig 1.1: Table showing the broad Search Engine Categories. Note the type that index web pages and those that index web sites.

The primary search engines have a few defined sub-types that are listed in Fig 1.2. Shopping, Multimedia and Kids orientated searches are also available on Google and Yahoo although most search engine users just operate from the very basic screen that they are first offered. There is a lot more on web behaviours later in the chapter.

1 Search Engine Overview

Froogle BETA **kelkoo** SHOPPING on YAHOO!

Sub-Type	Used For	Examples
Shopping	As the name suggests the focus is on retail therapy.	Froggle, Kelkoo, Nextag, Bizrate
Multimedia	These relatively new engines search for sounds and images.	Kazaa, Ditto, Picsearch.
Kids	Filtered results to keep kids safe on the Internet	Kidsclick, Yahooligans
Speciality	Topic specific	Firstgov, Radio Directory
Country Specific	Focus on sites within the national boundary	T-Online(Germany), Tiscali (Europe)

Fig 1.2: Examples of Niche Search Engines.

There are many search engines variants but they can all be classified into the broad categories shown in Figure 1.1. Many niche search engines (shown in Figure 1.2) take their results from one or more of the major search engines and then filter them to present a slightly different set of search results.

The BBC is a good example of this type of 'value adding' approach where human editors present a more ordered and filtered view of the search results provided by the robot driven search engines.

Search Engine League Tables

Web site owners are usually keen to know just which search engines really matter. After all you could spend many hours submitting your site manually or using one of the many automatic submission methods that are on offer and not know if your efforts had been successful. You are then left to wonder whether or when you should consider re-submitting your site as you don't want the search engine to blacklist you as a spammer!

Data is hard to come by and is often conflicting. I have seen reports that both Google and MSN host over 60% of searches between them relegating Yahoo to an also-ran! Other surveys make Yahoo! a key player, much more important than MSN. Commentators rate them in different ways but nearly everyone agrees that Google is now in the top place in the search engine league table. First place is a double edged sword as it means that Google is servicing a large proportion of the searches on the Internet but it is also crammed full of web sites with thousands more trying to join every day! This has forced Google to become ever more automated and it can be extremely difficult to achieve a workable balance between the human user of a web site and the robots that crawl through the site looking for links, keywords and so on.

It is difficult to measure how we search the Internet. The experts seem to be settling on using a measure called search hours, which is the time a person spends using a particular search engine. This is a good measure but unfortunately it does not tell us just how successful the searches have been! The web user may have spent many hours searching through web pages that have had little to do with the information that he was really after.

1 Search Engine Overview

The interlinking between search engines is also a factor and the alliances move around from time to time as acquisitions are made or a major player like MSN decides to get their results from another provider or to go it alone as they decided a short while ago. Many of the former innovators are now just minor search engines but getting your web pages indexed by them will still get your business or web site known by a large number of people.

Fig 1.3: The main direct or primary search engines.

6

Search Engine Overview 1

Direct Search Engines

Many long term users of the Internet have a preferred search engine such as Altavista or Lycos and will stick with it no matter what! Do remember that something like 500 million searches are carried out each day and a 0.3 % share still equates to 1.5 million searches per day. The big players from the last two or three years are shown in Figure 1.3. Do note who they are but also take a look at their market share in Figure 1.4 and how it has changed in just 2 or 3 years. In that short time Google has doubled its share mainly at the expense of Yahoo and MSN.

Search Engine	2003	2004	2005
Google	30	49	63
Yahoo!	30	16	13
msn	19	13	10
AOL	2	4	3
Ask Jeeves	1	1	1
altavista	1	0.5	0.3
Lycos	1	0.5	0.07
Netscape	0.5	0.3	0.16
Others	15.5	15.7	9.47

Fig 1.4: Search Engine Market Share gathered from a number of sources. Figures are the percentage of search traffic handled by a particular search engine.

1 Search Engine Overview

These are worldwide figures and within a particular market such as the UK or Canada Google's share may be as high as 70%. All web site owners want to achieve a top ranking in Google and we will explore this issue in depth in later chapters.

The top search engines (with the exception of AOL) are also acquiring the minor players and we are now seeing the emergence of the Google, Yahoo and Ask Jeeves search engine families. MSN is going it alone and AOL has partnered with Google. This now means that you don't really need to worry about submitting your web site manually to many minor search engines as there are just a few valuable input or access points to this huge network.

Many search engines get their data from other ones and rely on search directories to alert them to the presence of new sites that they don't detect themselves. It varies from continent to continent and we only have space to cover the USA and UK/Europe. The situation in Europe won't differ that much from that in the UK and you may find that one or two local ISPs like Tiscali have a significant share of local market.

Search Engine Relationships

It is important to keep in mind that the search engines are now in families and that this interlinking can explain why your position in several search engines seems to be in sync! It can also explain why your site is not appearing in search engine A – it may very well be that it takes its results from search engine B that is being particularly slow at updating its indexes because they may be simply overwhelmed with submissions and don't have enough resources to cope with the demand.

Search Engine Overview

Search Engine	Feeds primary results to these search engines		
msn			
YAHOO!	alltheweb	altavista	
Google	AOL	Netscape	
Ask Jeeves		LYCOS	iwon

Fig 1.5: Search Engine Relationships in the US.

Search Engine	Feeds primary results to these search engines			
msn				
YAHOO!	alltheweb	altavista	bbc.co.uk	
	BT Internet	wanadoo		
Google	AOL	Netscape	ntlworld.com	
Ask Jeeves		LYCOS		

Fig 1.6: The relationships in the UK search engine market are like that of the USA with the addition of several local portals.

1 Search Engine Overview

Figure 1.5 shows how the search engines 'feed off' one another in the United States. The same diagram is repeated in Fig. 1.6 for the United Kingdom where you can see the presence of some local search engines mainly provided by the major ISPs. The UK configuration is repeated across many European countries with Wanadoo, Lycos, AOL and Tiscali commanding a significant share of that local search market.

Exercise 1

1. *If your particular ISP is not listed in the tables then you can check for yourself where they are getting their search results from:*

    a. *First perform a visual check as there may be a statement on the website like this one from Tiscali.*

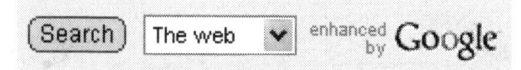

    b. *Run a very elaborate search by entering several words into the search box (possibly using the advanced option) and note the top 5 results (ignore the paid or sponsored listings at the top or along the side).*

    c. *Run the same search in the local search engine of Google and Yahoo. For the UK this is google.co.uk and yahoo.co.uk. One of them will be very similar and this will be where the results are being fed from.*

Search Engine Overview 1

Directory Search Engines

The search directories are like the Yellow Pages or other local paper directories and they give a concise description of a web site sorted by categories. Concise can mean as few as 60 characters for the site title and the main site description may have to fit into around 100 characters. The exercise of submitting your web site to one of these online directories really makes you think about what your web site is all about!

Many directories are run by human editors so you have to be courteous and considerate of their time by not giving them a poor web site to review. The big fish in all of this is the Open Directory project known as DMOZ or Directory Mozilla that is run on a volunteer basis. The fact that editors are using their spare time can make any submission process very slow and feedback on your progress is non-existent unless you get a very conscientious person who responds to all the queries in the forums.

Depending on an editor's workload you could wait many months for your submission to be processed. Getting listed in DMOZ is therefore a very slow process and some section editors have not added a new listing in over a year! The number of active editors is in slow decline and that means that the backlog increases and then more editors drop away. It is one of those situations that can quickly spiral out of control and I can foresee the eventual demise of DMOZ!

DMOZ really is a lottery. I have observed a slow decline in the importance of DMOZ over the past few years. Several leading Search Engine specialists now giving the same advice of not losing too much sleep of your web site fails to get listed.

1 Search Engine Overview

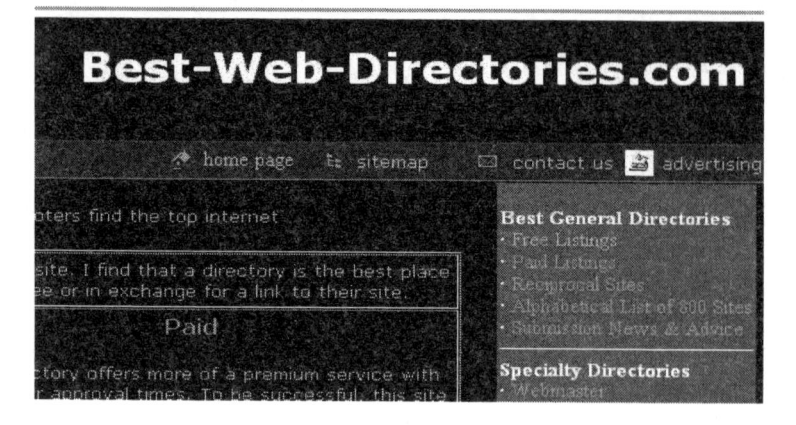

Fig 1.7: Here you can find a review of the most important Search Engine Directories. Point your browser at http://www.best-web-directories.com

LINKOPEDIA	www.linkopedia.com
Search Sight	www.searchsight.com
World Site Index	www.worldsiteindex.com
dmoz open directory project	www.dmoz.org

Fig 1.8: DMOZ and three alternative routes to getting an incoming link to your site.

Search Engine Overview 1

Luckily there are other directories to work with. The directories are an important resource as they provide **an external link** into your site. I will tell you a little bit later on why this is so important and how not to overdo things either. Search engines use many obvious and some not so obvious parameters to rate web sites. The 'sensitivity' of individual parameters is adjusted from time to time and a web site with a large number of low quality links may drop down the ratings.

I have found these three directories (see Figure 1.8) to be very efficient and an effective substitute for the sluggishness of DMOZ. Do note that some directories are free whilst others charge a hefty fee. I do recommend that you have a Paypal account handy as this will make the whole process simpler and stress free.

I recommend that you visit the list of directories in Figure 1.7 and choose a handful that fit in with the profile of your web site and your budget! Then visit those actual directories and just check who has actually listed their web sites with it. The directory may be trying to attract a certain type of web site so do carry out some thorough research before spending time going through the registration process. Combined with one or two niche directories from the resource in Figure 1.14 this will certainly be enough to get started. Later you may want to submit your web site to several other directories.

Search or Directory

Let me take just a few moments to illustrate the difference between the two types of search engines. We will use Google as our example. If you go to www.google.com or your local version then you will see a screen like Figure 1.9.

1 Search Engine Overview

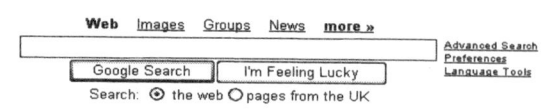

Fig 1.9: Google's primary search engine.

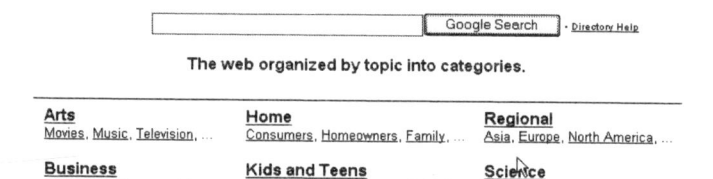

Fig 1.10: Google's directory search engine.

Search Engine Overview 1

However find the Google Directory (http://directory.google.com) and you will see quite a different picture as shown in Figure 1.10. The difference is that the familiar Google screen is what used to be called a 'Free Text' search, which means that you try to find things in quite a haphazard way.

The Google banner explains the Directory concept quite clearly:

The Web Organised by Topic into Categories.

Directory Relationships

One big directory sits at the heart of the Internet and as I have said it is a big problem! DMOZ or the open directory project feeds directory type results to Google, Lycos, Hotbot, AOL, Netscape, Altavista and many others.

[d][m][o][z] open directory project
about dmoz | s\

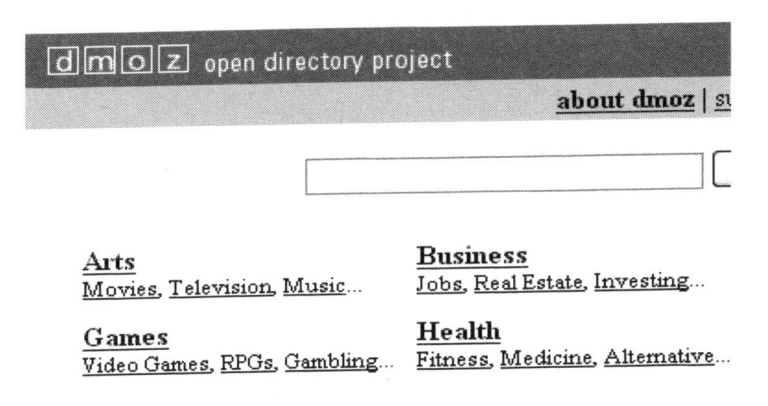

Arts
Movies, Television, Music...

Business
Jobs, Real Estate, Investing...

Games
Video Games, RPGs, Gambling...

Health
Fitness, Medicine, Alternative...

Fig 1.11: DMOZ is central in feeding search results to the directory portions of many search engines.

15

1 Search Engine Overview

The other big directory is provided by Yahoo which has its own system where web sites get charged a hefty $299 just to be reviewed by an editor and if included this becomes your annual renewal fee. Obviously this is not for everyone and do remember that there is no absolute guarantee that your entry will be accepted.

Fig 1.12: Yahoo and MSN search directories.

MSN has a small business directory (http://sbd.bcentral.com/) aimed mainly at the US business market but it may well expand this service to compete with Yahoo and Google. Within the UK Mirago is a big player but again charges a significant fee to include your web site in its directory. The question to ask yourself is just how important it is for your web site to be listed in these directories? Look at your own behaviour on the web as a good guide to just how many directories you need to use.

So far as can be determined at the moment the search engines like to find at least one qualified external link into a web site and this is the main reason for spending time on them!

Search Engine Overview 1

Pay per Click

There is yet another way to get a listing in the search engines and this is to pay the search engine provider to give you a high visibility listing above or to one side of the organic listings.

There are many names for this such as sponsored link, featured link, etc. Pay per Click costs vary wildly so don't rush in to the first provider you come across. My last survey of this sector listed over **640** such engines so caution is advised before rushing ahead. Several of the PPC engines that I have used have never produced any of the traffic levels promised.

Search Engine	Feeds paid for results to these search engines.			
YAHOO!	alltheweb find it all	altavista	msn	
	overture a YAHOO! company			
Google	AOL	Netscape network	iwon Over $60 million awarded!	
	TEOMA	LYCOS	Ask Jeeves	

Fig 1.13: PPC relationships driven by Google and Yahoo.

I think you should now have an appreciation of how the search engines and directories link together and probably have guessed that you don't need to poke every button to get your site noted and listed – just a few selective ones to start you off and then a programme of filling the gaps with PPC.

1 Search Engine Overview

Specialist Search Engines

The final type of search engine that I want to cover is called specialist or niche and is aimed at very small communities of users. The best list that I have found is at:

http://www.allsearchengines.com.

If you explore this site you will certainly find a myriad of specialist engines although it is often unclear how you would go about submitting your own URL to the various sites.

Fig 1.14: Your entry point to a myriad of niche search engines.

Search Engine Overview 1

Don't write specialist search engines off too quickly. I use one called the Radio Directory for my digital radio information publishing and it has brought a number of potential customers to the Radio Engineering web site. The best advice that I can give you is that if you can't find an obvious home for your web site then don't worry about it. Move on with a mental note to check back in a few months time. But don't forget that a listing will provide you with another qualified link into your website.

How Search Engines Index the Web

There is a well defined cycle that most of the search engines adhere to. Google has its own way of doing things and I will cover this shortly. Typically the updates within the search engines' indexes happen towards the end of the calendar month but don't be surprised to see the robots (automated processes that crawl through the web pages) dropping by on a more regular basis. Usually each robot has a name or other way of identifying it but there are a few that do not do this.

Each index is literally a huge database of cross-referenced entries between keywords or keyword phrases and web site pages that the search engine has ranked in order of their relevancy to the keyword and its synonyms. Note that the use of synonyms in web pages is growing in importance.

Don't forget that the objective of each search engine is to return those web pages that most closely or exactly satisfy the query typed in by the web user. The big four (Google, Yahoo, MSN & ASK) are becoming more selective about which pages they index and there is a trend towards testing out new web sites with insignificant searches before including the web page in the main index.

1 Search Engine Overview

From time to time the search engines also update their search algorithms (the processes that determine the ranking of web pages within the index) and during the weeks after such upgrades web pages can appear and disappear at random. MSN, Yahoo and Google all carried out major upgrades in the second half of 2005.

Once your site gets added to the index the search engines want to ensure that:

- The web pages are still relevant.

- Your relative scoring or ranking hasn't changed as a result of any new data or information that you may have added since the last time they visited. These updates may have made your web page more or less relevant in comparison to other web pages that will also have changed in that time.

Some robots drop by just once a month; others can appear every week and download varying amounts of data from your site. I will show you in a later chapter how to access and understand the log files that contain this and other useful information. I will also show you how to check how these robots are processing the data picked up from your site.

You may find it a worthwhile exercise to make a log of these visits for a short time as a way of learning how the robots behave.

The search engines go through a number of stages before you get a stable listing in their indexes. There are various names for these stages but they fall into the four phases listed below.

Search Engine Overview 1

1. Detection – the robot that crawls or 'spiders' the Internet has to find your site and when they do you may find that your pages are listed just because the site is new. Google is particularly guilty of this and they raise your hopes too much in the first month only to dash them later on!!

2. Evaluation – Another/different robot is likely to visit your site with a view to putting the pages into the main index.

3. Acceptance – Hopefully the pages have now been processed and stored in the main index.

4. Updating – When the Search Engine has put your web pages in its index it will revisit from time to time to check for changes to your site.

During the first three stages the revisions to the search engines' listings or indexes occur at the month end. Updating can happen at any time during a month.

Important Note

This means that just getting your web site a stable listing (where your web pages are being used as search results) by a search engine could take three months. With Google it could take six to eight months of continuous work.

Once a site has been accepted then updates such as new pages get added in a matter of days rather than months. You then find that search engine robots visit your web pages several times a month.

1 Search Engine Overview

The Google Index

Google seems to have evolved an elaborate system to evaluate new web sites. Some search commentators have called this the 'Google Sandbox'. The term 'Sandbox' is typically used for a parallel computer system that users can learn on without any fear of making mistakes that lose data or cause corruption.

It can now take 6 to 8 months or longer for Google to incorporate a new site into its major index. The process starts with Google's first contact with a web site so it may be worthwhile submitting the URL to Google just as soon as the majority of the web pages have crossed the quality threshold set in the next chapter. Google will visit your web pages and note them for future visits but will not add any of them to the index at that time.

After a little while, Google will index the web pages and use them for some of the less important queries. The pages can also move in and out of the index throughout this period. Google has apparently adopted this approach so that webmasters build quality content rather than influence their ranking by using a network of micro-sites that provide an artificial boost to a web site's popularity. There doesn't seem to be any way to speed up this process other than to continue creating good quality content. It is also important not to get sidetracked by Google and forget about MSN and Yahoo.

A good strategy to get your web site maximum visibility is to optimise a few pages for each search engine. This does involve creating a good data architecture that has your content in well thought out pages that link seamlessly with one another.

Ranking

Throughout this chapter, I have been referring to the ranking given to a web page. When you use an Internet search engine (SE) the SE returns a number of Search Engine Results Pages (SERP) in response to your query. Each page usually has 10 web pages listed in a ranked order: page 1 lists web pages 1-10; page 2 has web pages 11-21 and so on until all the results have been displayed. This is not about the related topic of the Google PageRank algorithm but the general way that search engines return results to queries.

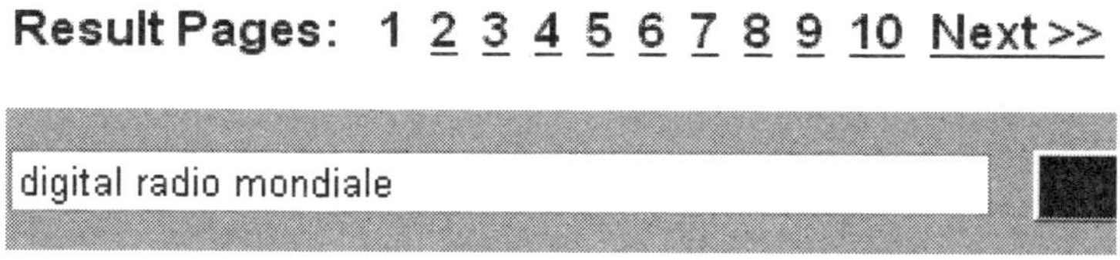

Result Pages: 1 2 3 4 5 6 7 8 9 10 Next >>

digital radio mondiale

Fig 1.15: Part of an Altavista SERP.

Web Behaviour

Achieving a top 10 or top 20 ranking in a search engine but particularly in Google is the holy grail of the Search Engine Optimisation (SEO) industry that now has many experts all claiming to be able to achieve that high ranking.

We will see later that many of these assertions are bogus or the actions that achieve a temporary high ranking are liable to sanction by the search engines.

1 Search Engine Overview

According to various strands of research most people who use search engines get turned off by having to scan for any length of time through the search results and rarely get beyond two pages of them (1-20).

Personally I think that many people go well beyond this 2 page limit if they really have to find a particular piece of information. For casual surfing or shopping then I agree that this is probably true. According to research conducted by a University in the USA, users of the web typically only visit the first three web sites thrown up by their query and then 20% of the same surfers will spend less than a minute deciding whether any of the documents are relevant for them! I think that we would agree that people make quick judgements about a web site in that if they don't quickly spot something of interest they will hit the Back button on their browser. People also don't want to wait too long for a page to load.

Search Behaviour

The Penn State's School of Information Sciences and Technology (IST) conducted tests where they found that half of all users entered only one query term or single key word with 54 percent viewing just one page of results in each session (a session is a query or series of queries submitted by a user during one interaction with a Web search engine). Only an additional 19 percent went on to the second page in sessions, and fewer than 10 percent of users bothered with the third page of results. A similar drop-off in numbers occurred when the researchers considered how many results the searchers viewed per query. About 55 percent of users checked out one result only. More than 80 percent stopped after looking at three results.

Search Engine Overview 1

In summary users took quite a lazy approach to searching and reviewing. This survey was at a time when there was less focused use of the internet so perhaps things have changed in the last few years?

A more recent study carried out by Cornell University tried to take this research a bit further by again measuring user behaviour when presented with a page of results in response to entering a query.

The queries were not seen as the important factor so a mix of single and multi-word phrases was used. The study reached four really valuable conclusions:

- Users place substantial trust in the search engines' ability to determine the relevance of the returned results list. For example, if Google returns a certain web page as number 1 then users are more likely to click on that page.

- Users also scan the results page and form a judgement on the overall quality of returned search results. A low quality score will cause users either to abandon the whole search or to selectively pick through the results and maybe even move to other pages.

- Users judge the quality of the link being offered up and ignore it if it doesn't seem relevant. For example say that a user has entered the search term of 'tomatoes' and two of the links returned were 'www.freds.co.uk/garden.htm' and 'www.freds-garden-centre.co.uk/tomato-plants.htm'. The study showed that the user would give more credibility to the second link and click on that one.

1 Search Engine Overview

- Users seemed to work linearly through the returned results list but at times looked at every other result. For example many users looked at result 3 and then at result number 5 rather than number 4.

With more businesses opting to market through search engines rather than ads, those percentages from the Penn State and Cornell studies illustrate why a high ranking on a major Web search engine can make the difference between commercial success and failure.

The Cornell study also emphasised how important the web page's abstract or summary can be as a factor in influencing a user's choices. A well written site abstract or description that appears on the results page can direct more users to a site -- provided the description is enticing and relevant specifics about the site are included.

Both studies show that as good as the search engines are there is room for improvement. Niche search engines that focus on a narrow topic or search engines that cluster results by finding similarities and grouping them may be consumers' best bet for improving relevancy but we are a long way away from that position. Google is trying out many techniques to find ways to improve relevancy. Unfortunately, some of their initiatives will have a negative effect on new web sites as the time between detection and acceptance into the main index will continue to increase.

I think we all know that this erratic behaviour is the way any casual surfer works. I also know that if I am looking for something that is really important to me then I dig deeper and deeper, try new searches and different combinations of keywords and finally move to another search engine before I give up.

Search Engine Overview 1

These studies also show the real benefit of preparing your web pages to the standards required by the top search engines. Adhering to these standards means that your pages and site structure will be of a high quality and portray your business in the best possible way to your customers.

Important Note

A search engine often creates its own abstract or description for your web page rather that reading your title or web page description. There is usually some reason why this has happened and it is an indication of how well the robot managed to work its way through your web site.

Google PageRank

I think that I am correct in saying that the concept of PageRank was conceived by Google. Search Engines are continually looking for new ways to differentiate one site from another. Google devised PageRank as a way of measuring a page's importance. PageRank is a complicated process and many experts are unsure if Google or others now use it in a significant way. Nevertheless optimising a site so each page generates a high PageRank is still a good thing. To start out, each page in a web site has a ranking value that is determined by its content, structure and other parameters. As pages within the web site are linked together the PageRank gets redistributed and some pages end up with a higher value than their neighbours. Add in links to other sites and the PageRank of each page alters again.

1 Search Engine Overview

To help you understand this concept a bit more you should get access to the Google Toolbar (http://toolbar.google.com) and install it. You may have to go into 'Options' and enable the PageRank feature. The PageRank for that particular page will appear as a green bar graph. Hover the mouse over it and you get a message like the one in Figure 1.16: PageRank is Google's measure of the importance of this page (6/10).

Fig 1.16: Google Tool Bar.

The toolbar is a very coarse measure of the actual page ranking that can vary between 0 and several million and is expressed as a value between 0 and 10 on a logarithmic scale. The value on the toolbar probably only relates to the internal Google algorithm rather than accurately representing the value your web page really has in the index.

Important Note

Use the toolbar indication as a guide only. There is no real evidence that the number given is actually used by Google in deciding to offer up a particular web page in response to a search query.

Search Engine Overview 1

The use of a logarithmic scale does mean that it gets progressively more difficult to move up the page ranking scale the higher you get. To move from PR1 to PR2 takes a small increase whilst to move from PR3 to PR4 is much more difficult and to get from PR8 to PR9 is extremely difficult.

PageRank is concerned with links to other web sites and pages within your site. There will be three areas of linkage:

1. Links to your site from other web sites

2. Links from your site to other web sites

3. The Internal navigational links within your site.

PageRank is bi-directional, meaning that the external web pages that you link to can take value away from your pages – this is called 'leaking page rank'.

All the search engines refer to the importance of external links to your site. Getting a listing in a directory that is edited by humans qualifies as a link from another site to yours and will help your ranking in Google. To be very honest with you I am just not sure if it is as helpful as some people make out. That is why when I use minor directories I opt for one paid for link and then free listings after that. Changes in the way the search engines rank web pages has shifted the focus to 'quality' links that have a similar theme to your web site.

The goalposts will continue to move and you must keep up with these developments to maintain your web site's place in the rankings.

1 Search Engine Overview

Checklist 1

Visit one or more of these web sites to sign up for their Search Engine newsletters. There are thousands of web sites and forums on the topic but I can recommend these as providers of good quality information.

From Axandra:

http://www.free-seo-news.com/index.php

From Search Engine Watch:

http://searchenginewatch.com/

Follow the newsletter link where you then have a choice of either Searchday or the Search Engine Report.

From the Webmasters World:

http://www.webmastersworld.com

Subscribe to their weekly summary of developments

From the Webmaster's Reference:

http://www.webreference.com

Subscribe to either (or both) the daily and weekly summaries. This one is a bit more technical but usually has a good section on search engines. I would recommend that you go for the weekly or monthly summaries as you can get overwhelmed with information very quickly and never read them.

Search Engine Overview 1

Exercise 2

Here are a few things that you should do before starting on Chapter 2.

- *Choose a handful of general directories where your web site seems 'at home' and aligns with other web sites in that particular category. Keep this list for use in chapter 3.*

- *Spend about an hour researching DMOZ. If, at the end of that period, you have not found the appropriate category for your web site then I would just forget it!*

- *Find at least one niche directory as this type of search directory is growing in importance.*

- *Sign up to some sources of search engine news so that you are increasing your understanding of this industry.*

Summary

- There are just four major search engines: Google, Yahoo, MSN and Ask. These search engines feed results to many other search engines.

- Search directories provide an important incoming link to your web site.

- PageRank is Google's way of assessing the importance of a web page.

1 Search Engine Overview

Next Chapter

Now that you have a good understanding of how the whole Internet search engine environment works we will move on to learning how to influence the various search engines so that your web pages are as prominent or visible as possible.

You must have a fairly good website up and running before you submit it to the search engines and directories otherwise both the human reviewers and the automatic crawlers are going to just mark it as not worth bothering with. Remember to make Google top of the list.

In the next chapter I will show you how to give your web site a health check. You can then spruce up your site so that the Search Engines do index it and add it to their lists of important URLs.

2. Web Site Improvements

This chapter aims to help you eliminate the major issues that will prevent your web site being accepted into a search engine index. In a sense this is a type of low level optimization but I believe that a web site has to first cross a **quality threshold** before the owner begins the process of improving it.

Web Site Health Check

Before you begin the process of reviewing and changing your web site to make it more search engine friendly you need to be aware of some of the reasons why search engines may bypass a web site completely. These problems can have a dramatic and instant effect or an intermittent one where web pages come and go in an index, but in either case it is worth just checking these issues off one by one before proceeding with the more detailed work on your web site.

Important Note

If you are improving or changing any web site then you must always be sure that you can reverse out your changes and go back to the previous working version. Use some sort of versioning that make sense to you such as website_v1, then website_v1A for minor changes and then onto website_v2 for the next major update and so on. If you make a mistake, or your web site authoring tool throws a wobbly then you will only lose a certain amount of work.

2 Web Site Improvements

Minimum Amount of Content

First of all you need to have created a certain amount of content before submitting a web site to both the search engines and search directories. As a general rule of thumb your web site should have an absolute minimum of 5 pages and ideally around 8 pages with about 400-500 words per page.

This minimum number of pages allows you to create enough internal links to influence your rating or ranking in the search engine. It also means that the human editors will take your site seriously and add it to their directories. Over time your site will grow and double or triple in size but you should definitely have some 3000 to 5000 words of good, well written, content in your web site before getting the search engines to look at it.

Important Note

Given the way Google now seems to operate I would consider submitting the web site URL to them as soon as you reach the lower limit.

If your web site is of or around the size that I mentioned then I would recommend that you don't add any more content or pages until I have shown you how to structure the existing data to create a high visibility web site.

Do remember that the process of changing a web site to be more 'search engine friendly' takes several months to complete and then you need to start the process all over again, thankfully at somewhat reduced level of effort, to maintain your place in the rankings. Once you get the hang of the process the whole task becomes a lot easier and you will be able to make updates in next to no time.

Web Site Improvements 2

Don't worry too much if your site page and word counts are below these recommendations or that you have already submitted the URL to the search engines a number of times to try to get them to notice it.

It may now take a bit longer overall but any negative effects can be put right over time.

Robots & Humans

A web site can slip down the rankings just as it can come and go in the listings within some search engines. The best advice that I can give, is to always wait for the next update as indexing errors do occur from time to time and the status quo is likely to be restored within a short time. On occasions a particular search engine (this will usually be Google!) will stubbornly refuse to rank your web site for no apparent reason (that you can determine!). You have to persevere and keep chipping away at Google to make things happen.

For the majority of web sites, listing problems come down to having web pages that are easy and attractive for the human viewer to use and browse but difficult for the robot sent by the search engines.

Here are a few of the top robot versus human issues:

Too Many Images

Search engines use text to index your site. If your web pages are mainly graphical, which means that you have lots and lots of pictures and graphics with little accompanying text then you are likely to have a few problems with the search engines.

2 Web Site Improvements

There are a number of minor things that you can do to improve matters such as using certain HTML tags to provide descriptions of the images but the bottom line is that you need to add more text to your web site.

You also have to make sure that if you are using visual links within images there is also text that provides the same information both for the robot and the visually impaired human user who is using special software to 'read' your web pages.

You can achieve this in three ways:

- Making sure that the 'ALT' tag of each image has one of your keyword phrases as well as text that actually describes the image. It is important that this rule is followed for the first image tag on the page.*

- Breaking the images up with small text boxes either below or to one side of a group of images.

- Offering a text-only version of the site if this can be achieved. It just won't be a practical answer for many sites.

You may have to do some extra work to comply with the new accessibility guidelines that aim to make web sites accessible to every web user, even those that have a physical impairment of some kind. Any text that you add to describe an image must be meaningful and not just full of keywords.

* If you use a graphical web page creation tool or work with templates it is likely that many of the graphics such as heavy lines are actually images with no ALT tag text. Here, there is no point in describing the image so you may as well use it with a relevant keyword phrase.

Web Site Improvements 2

Using Frames

A web site with frames can usually be identified visually by it having a number of slider bars that scroll independently of each other. Frames are attractive to web designers as they allow multiple HTML documents to be displayed as separate windows that operate independently of each other.

```
<!DOCTYPE HTML PUBLIC "-//W3C//DTD HTML 4.01
Frameset//EN">
<HTML LANG="EN">
<HEAD>
<TITLE>A demo of a frameset document</TITLE>
</HEAD>
<FRAMESET cols="25%, 75%">
    <FRAMESET rows="200, 200">
        <FRAME src="frame1.html">
        <FRAME src="frame2.gif">
    </FRAMESET>
    <FRAME src="frame3.html">
<NOFRAMES>
<P>if you are reading this section then your
browser does not support frames. This frameset
document contains: <UL>
<LI><A href="frame1.html">Good content  </A>
<LI><IMG src=" frame2.gif" alt="An image">
<LI><A href="frame3.html">Some other
content</A></UL>
    </NOFRAMES>
  </FRAMESET>
  </HTML>
```

Fig 2.1: Source code of a frameset document. Note that there are 'FRAME src' and 'IMG src' links in the code.

2 Web Site Improvements

The layout of the views or sub-windows is specified in a special HTML document called a Frameset. This type of document has a different structure to normal HTML documents and this is declared at the top of the document. You can check for this by using the option in your browser to view the source code of the web page. You should see code similar to that shown in Figure 2.1. The source code may be a lot more complicated than this simple example so use the edit functions in Notepad to search for the keywords of FRAME and FRAMESET.

A normal HTML document or page has a HEAD and BODY section that are indexed by the Search Engine; the Frameset document or page has a HEAD section and a FRAMESET instead of the BODY.

The problem is that the search engines treat this page as a basic HTML document and do not follow the 'links' to the actual frames specified within the document. The links in the case of a FRAMESET document are provided by 'SRC' tags rather than 'HREF' ones. Google claims that it can handle frames to some extent but still advocates that a single web page should really correspond to a single URL. With frames this is not true as the frameset can expand out to many pages.

Yahoo agrees with Google and states that their robot only follows HREF links rather than the SRC links used in frames. The options open to you are to redesign the site without frames. If this is not possible then you could use a <NOFRAMES> section to add a description of the site together with some other content for the search engines to index as shown in Figure 2.1 above.

For more clarity you can include a pair of <BODY></BODY> tags inside the <NOFRAMES> ones but they are not technically required.

Web Site Improvements 2

There are three important points to remember:

- Older browsers that cannot handle frames will display the NOFRAMES sections so do make it readable. By using a text only browser (Lynx) you can check that your code is being displayed correctly and will be seen by the search engine robot.

- Some search engines will index the frameset pages and offer them up to users as individual web pages. This could strand the user with no way back to your main site: make sure that there are explicit links within each frameset page to where you want users to go.

- The search engine spiders that can handle framesets will show the individual pages rather than the frameset. This may not be what you want.

The best recommendation is that you should avoid frames if you possibly can. Only use them if you really know what you are doing. On a positive note more and more search engine robots are starting to handle frames.

If you are not sure then check the help pages of the particular search engine. Figure 2.2 confirms that the ASK search engine will follow 'SRC' tags.

Q: What types of links does the Ask.com crawler follow?
A: The Ask.com crawler will follow HREF links, SRC links and re-directs.

Fig 2.2: The ASK help centre confirms that they are able to handle frames.

2 Web Site Improvements

Search Engine	SRC links
Google	Yes
ASK	Yes
Yahoo	No
MSN	No
AllTheWeb	No
Altavista	No

Fig 2.3: Search engines that state that they can follow 'SRC' links as well as 'HREF' ones.

Dynamically Generated Web Pages

A dynamically generated web page is one that is created 'on the fly' in response to a stimulus or input such as a database query. Most search engines, with the exception of Google and those driven by the Inktomi search engine, cannot handle the very large URLs generated by this dynamic process. Google however is wary of generating too many dynamic pages as they could gobble up your bandwidth or even crash the site. I have had this problem with Alexa and only the understanding of my hosting company prevented my web site going 'black' for two weeks. Alexa's explanation was that their robot got itself in a loop trying to extract dynamic content and used up 100s of megabytes of bandwidth.

My own experience is that Google likes dynamically generated pages and will fill up its index with them at the expense of the content that I really wanted it to add to its index. You may have to prevent search engines from going into Forums and Online Stores as both typically use MySQL databases to store data.

Web Site Improvements 2

The recommendation is that you should add as many 'static' HTML pages around your dynamic ones as you can and consider using the robots file to control the search engines.

Using Free Hosting Space

Many ISPs offer a generous amount of free web space for personal or even business use. Some search engines impose a limit on the number of pages they will index from a single domain and others are adopting a policy of not even bothering to crawl them.

At the moment Google continues to 'crawl' the well known community sites such as Geocities. Data about the other three major search engines is contradictory so the best recommendation that I can give is to acquire your own domain name and hosting space from a reputable provider.

Complicated Web Pages

Search robots are evolving all the time but in general they are behind the times so far as web development is concerned. If your web pages use Macromedia Flash intros, DHTML, extensive JavaScript or password controlled access then it is likely that the robots will encounter problems.

The recommendation is that you test your site using a text-only browser link Lynx (http://lynx.browser.org) and see how it copes with your web site. Redesign out or eliminate any problem areas.

There is more information on Lynx in chapter 6.

41

2 Web Site Improvements

URL with Special Characters

It is rare, but do check that your web site's URL's do not contain the characters that are often found in dynamically generated web pages. These characters are '**&**', '**$**',' **=**', '**%**', and '**?**'.

You need to get rid of these characters if they are present in any of your page URLs. This is unusual but it is worth viewing all your pages in a browser and check just what does appear in the address bar. If you are using bought-in scripts in Perl or PHP then I strongly advise that you carry out this check.

Welcome Page

Is your welcome page really necessary? Search engines can get 'confused' and they just won't follow the link to the real content. If you are having problems consider removing the welcome page just to check if it is having a negative effect.

Deep Pages

Most spiders only crawl two levels down in the directory structure on a web site. Google crawls a bit deeper but no one is quite sure how deep this is. To be safe you should publish your web site in a **flat structure** rather than in a **site structure** that will replicate how you have linked your pages in a parent child relationship.

Old Pages

It is worth checking your web site to make sure that all the files are current. If the spider determines that many of the pages are old then your web pages will get a low score in the index.

Web Site Improvements 2

Flash Pages

The eye-catching intro is now very common and it leads the human viewer forward to similar pages that can be navigated visually. Apart from Google, and there is some doubt even about this, most search engines cannot deal with Flash or Shockwave files. You should offer a non-flash version of your web pages for accessibility and indexing reasons.

Hidden Text

This is one of the ways of spamming a search engine but you can blunder into it by accident. Hidden or invisible text use characters that are the same colour as the background. Humans can't see it but the spiders find it. However, you can innocently make this happen by having a section of your web page, such as a table, with the background of the cells in a particular colour (imagine it is blue for the moment). If you then give the text within that cell the same colour as the overall page background colour (imagine this is white), everything looks fine – but the spider may ignore the cell formatting information and incorrectly determine that you have hidden text! For this reason I rarely use any text colour other than black.

Hosting Problems

These can vary from poor uptime to restricted bandwidth that can result in a slow response time that affects the robots' activity. If you are concerned about uptime, then carry out some research or move to a host with a good reputation. A big hosting company is also likely to have masses of bandwidth that will mean fast response times.

2 Web Site Improvements

Valid HTML Code

This can be one of the most overlooked areas as many of us rely on graphical web page generators. The biggest problem that I have found is that some of them don't close HTML tags properly.

There are many HTML validation software packages and online services. My recommendation is that you use the one provided by the W3C organisation as they are the controlling body for the HTML family of languages. Point your browser at this URL: http://validator.w3.org/, input the full URL of your page, select the correct standard and you will then get a comprehensive analysis of your web page.

Be prepared for a fairly large list of actual errors and warnings and then see if you can fix some of them.

The report shown in Figure 2.4 looks very concerning. A closer analysis showed that there were 4 warnings (INFO) and of the remaining 14 issues, 10 are internal tags generated by the web page creation package (NetObjects Fusion 8). There are four real problems, and all of them are again as a result of the web site creation package not working to the standard:

- Missing end or closing </H2> header tag
- Missing end or closing </H3> header tag
- Orphan end of paragraph tag </P>.

I know that I can correct these by manually adding them as additional HTML code. The other errors with probably have to remain and I don't believe that they are causing the search engines too many problems.

Web Site Improvements 2

Fig 2.4: A web page failing with 18 errors. Not all of them are fatal errors so check the report carefully.

Redirection

This used to be an issue but I think that most search engines are happy to be re-directed from a 'placeholder' page to another web site. Altavista seems to be the exception to the rule. Again there are ways to be absolutely sure that the spider does not misinterpret the situation. I recommend three ways to achieve a 'safe' redirect but just two of them are practical for the majority of web site owners.

45

2 Web Site Improvements

Use a META tag as follows:

<meta http-equiv ="REFRESH" CONTENT ="0;
url=http://www.newsite.com/thispage.html" >

This generates the equivalent of a HTTP 301 code that directs the browser or spider to a new page.

Use a short PHP file like this:

```
<?php
header ("location: http://www.newsite.com/thispage.html");
?>
```

This method only works if this code is the very first output to the browser. If other PHP header information has gone out then this won't work.

Use the .htaccess file

You can use or create an '.htaccess' file but I do not recommend doing this unless you know exactly what you are doing.

Note on Checklists

You will encounter many checklists throughout this chapter and they will build up into a comprehensive list for you to work through. I write the lists in two ways: with a negative slant so that you can use the checklist as an aide memoir, or with a positive slant and you might like to use this type of checklist as a 'to-do' list.

Web Site Improvements 2

Checklist 2

- I have yet to create about 4000 words of content, organised into 5 to 8 pages.

- I am relying heavily on images to provide visual links with on-the-page content down below 200 to 300 words.

- I am using frames.

- I am using dynamically generated pages.

- I am using free hosting space with a very unmemorable URL that tells a web user very little about the content.

- I am using Flash Intros or extensive JavaScript or Dynamic HTML.

- The URL(s) of one or many of my web pages contains special characters.

- I use a welcome page.

- My hosting company is not reliable.

- I have validated the code of every page and found many significant errors.

- I have old or deep pages that need attention.

2 Web Site Improvements

Create a High Ranking Web Site

Having checked off or eliminated what might be seen as the more obscure issues it is now time to focus on the things that really need work. Don't forget that some of the items in the previous checklist may also generate a considerable amount of work for you.

Important Note

The way to be in the top ten of every internet search engine is to have your web pages full of well structured and unique content. The web pages themselves also need to be structured together in a logical manner.

This section of chapter 2 shows you how to introduce a minimum level of quality (a threshold) to your web site and web pages.

Whether you are trying to get that initial listing or you want to maintain or improve on a current ranking position, requires that you repeat a process of:

- Reviewing the state of your web pages in a critical but productive way. One of the secrets of creating a good web site is learning how to be objective. You can also get feedback from family and friends to help you make those critical judgements.

- Setting you (and your web site!) achievable objectives based on solid information.

Web Site Improvements 2

- Making changes to each of those pages to bring each one more in line with best practice and with known search engine requirements. Check also that the changes meet your objectives as well.

- Adding more content on a regular basis in a positive way that enhances a web page. Some search engines can equate a major change in content as a negative factor that indicates a change in ownership or worse as a sinister change in function.

- Always analysing the effects of those changes by whatever means available to you.

- Periodically starting the whole process from scratch again.

- Tackling any stubborn search engine in a planned way as you may make a small gain in that engine at the expense of several others.

- Possibly accepting that you have hit the point of diminishing returns where to move up another place in the rankings is just not worth the continuing effort.

You must be practical and methodical in everything that you do as haphazard changes will have detrimental effects.

Always remember that you are trying to remove anything that might block the robots extracting information from the web pages while providing human beings with an interesting web site.

2 Web Site Improvements

Crossing the Quality Threshold

The first objective is to cross that quality threshold, above which the search engines start to take notice of your web site. The underlying process that we will take each of your web pages through is cyclical and has three stages:

- **Review** the structure of the web site against the optimum design. Initially we will use a manual process. Later on I will introduce you to software tools that help with the more mechanical side of the analysis.

- From that review create an **action plan** consisting of tasks that need to be done. These actions need to be added to any checklist actions that you have.

- Those **changes** are applied to the web site and possibly to individual web pages.

- The effect of the changes is **reviewed** again to begin another cycle. The changes will produce both positive and negative results and you need to work out and note what these are telling you about your web site.

Step 1: Web Site Review

The first step is to review the web site as an entity. At this stage put the content of the web site to one side and instead look at the number of pages and the titles of those pages. It may help you to sketch this out as a simple diagram on a large sheet of paper so that you can add other details later on.

Web Site Improvements 2

Step 1A - Web Site Architecture

This is literally every aspect of your web site and your knowledge of this will build up as you work your way through this book. However there are a few, perhaps obvious points, that you should note at this early stage.

Navigation Structure

This is about the navigation menus that you offer to users – they will also be followed by the spiders as they are essentially internal page links. There are several ways to set up your navigation structure:

- First level – always provides links to those pages on the level below the home page.

- Parent level – links to the pages in the level above the current page.

- Current level – links to all pages that share the same parent page.

- Child level – links to the child pages of the current page.

- Breadcrumbs trail – displays a navigation tree all the way back to the home page.

- Ad-hoc – made up of selective pages.

If you can achieve it then the most search engine friendly method to use is a breadcrumbs trail.

2 Web Site Improvements

You need to consider the **entry points** or **landing pages,** where web users are most likely to enter your site. You won't actually know this until you gather some statistics from your web host but potential landing pages should all contain some basic information:

- A full navigation option provided by a separate menu at the top or bottom of the page. Ideally this should be a text menu.

- What the page is about.

- Who you are.

File Names & Extensions

If possible file names and any file directories should be constructed using keywords. If more than one keyword is used then the word should be hyphenated.

File extensions that are really safe to use are '.htm', '.html' and '.txt'. It should also be safe to use '.shtml' for secure web pages but stick with the tried and trusted extensions if you can. Images should be '.jpg', '.jpeg', '.png' or '.gif'.

You should be able to have '.pdf' and '.doc' files indexed as well but not every spider can deal with them correctly. I have had Google correctly index a PDF file and produce a load of incoherent text from an almost identical file. You just won't know until you see the results in the search engine.

To be safe I nearly always point the search engines at a HTML version of the PDF documents on the web site and just offer the PDF version as a download.

Web Site Improvements 2

Site Map

Consider having a site map that is available from the Home page. A site map is a list of links to all other pages and documents on your web site.

The purpose of a site map is twofold:

- It directs the robots to the content rich pages. This is most important for a highly or deeply linked site.

- It directs human viewers to the pages that you don't want the robots to bother with – 'contact' and 'about' pages.

The site map should obey the following guidelines:

- Use the same HTML template as the other pages.

- Each link should be keyword rich but relevant to the target page.

- The link should go directly to the page it refers to.

- Put 15-20 words of text that has been extracted from the target page next to each link as a summary.

- Keep keyword density to normal levels if you can, so that the page is not seen as search engine spam.

- Split the listing across several pages if you have a lot of pages and documents.

2 Web Site Improvements

This concept is slightly different to Google's Sitemap technology that uses XML. Google will use its own Sitemap **and** a HTML site map so make sure that they are in sync or that you have blocked the Googlebot from accessing the HTML page containing the visual site map.

Step 1B - Web Site Theme

I now want to introduce you to a very important concept in web site design, which is called the **theme** of a web site. The theme can be defined as the main topic or the recurring subjects than run through the whole site.

The theme of a web site and of individual pages is becoming more important to the internet search engines. They see it as a new way to find relevant web pages that are based mostly on content. If the determining factor can be mainly on content then many of the current optimization practices will be made ineffectual. Google is known to have acquired one or maybe two companies that specialise in this field.

I predict that this will become the main determining factor for web page ranking within two to three years.

Exercise 3

Write down on a piece of paper in ideally just one or two words the main topic (theme) of your web site.

Put simply state what your web site is all about.

Web Site Improvements 2

One of the biggest benefits of having a theme running all the way through your web site is that it will encourage you to keep it well organised. Sticking with your theme will then force you to keep your updates and changes consistent with that theme and stop your site growing in a haphazard way and losing an overall focus and consistency.

Evidence is emerging that Google is now developing techniques that analyse the whole page and even related pages in the same web site to determine the overall theme – this process may or may not involve the page's keywords. Yahoo and MSN are also heading in this direction as all three search engines attempt to be as relevant as possible to the web searcher.

Fact 1: You must have a theme and you must be ruthless in adhering to that theme.

Take some time now to check that you carried out Exercise 3 as thoroughly as possible and have truly identified the theme of your web site. It is very easy to assume what the theme is and have all the content supporting a very different one!

Exercise 4

If you haven't done so already list the titles of all the web pages in your web site. The title is what appears at the top of your web browser. See Figure 2.5.

Click on each individual page and note what the browser tells you.

2 Web Site Improvements

Fact 2: Remember that the search engines list and index the pages within your web site and not the site itself.

Fig 2.5: The title of your web page as seen by the web browser and the search engines.

Look closely at the page titles in your web site. Are you competing with millions of other pages called 'Frequently Asked Questions', 'Contact' and 'Home' and working hard to make them interesting?

Usually you have to have these pages so that the human visitor knows how to do certain things or post an order to an address, but don't spend too much time on trying to make your page called 'FAQs' outshine all other pages called by the same name! There are literally millions of them and you are basically wasting your valuable time.

Remember that as a web site creator you should always aim for a themed site as this means that it will be well thought out and visitors will return to it again and again.

The theme should be carried and developed in the main information pages and not in the ancillary ones such as the Contact or FAQ pages.

Web Site Improvements 2

If you can, make sure that the theme of each page overlaps with that of other pages and that all the pages contribute the web site's theme.

Checklist 3

This checklist will help you review the important points of the last few pages.

- I have completed exercise 1 and I don't have a theme for my web site.

- I have reviewed all my page titles and I need to change one or more of them.

- I have a number of page titles that will be common to millions of other web pages. I will make sure that they contain just low level information.

- I have identified some new pages that I need to create to reinforce the theme of the web site.

- I have some web pages that have little or nothing to contribute to the overall web site theme and that should be removed from the web site.

- I have isolated or orphan pages that loosely connect to the web site's theme but do not overlap with the sub-themes in the other pages. I will review them.

- I have poor and/or inconsistent navigation throughout the web site.

2 Web Site Improvements

- I do not have a site map on the home page.
- The site map does not follow the guidelines.
- The file names are not using keywords.
- The file extensions do not comply with the list given.

Notes

Practical Example

For the purpose of illustrating the next stage of this chapter I am going to refer to a web site called Cead Books that I created to link into a well known book seller. You can view the site at http://www.cead-books.co.uk if you want, but it is not necessary as the programme of changes that I will tell you about has already been applied to the site.

Just for the record the web site was built using a creation tool provided by the hosting company. The basic tool has its limitations in that you can only create 8 web pages and cannot easily create external links but nevertheless it allowed me to test out the many of the theories put forward about page size and other factors that affect search engine rankings in a very controlled environment.

My thinking in using such a tool was that if the theory worked here then by extension it should work in web site creation environments where there is much more control over all the elements.

Step 1C - Logical Structure

The first point to note is that the overall structure of the web site is extremely important and that it must connect or hang together in a logical format. Any visitor, either human or robotic must be able to navigate easily around the web site. I have already covered the need to have an overall theme and sub-themes that are inter-related that are distributed across your main information pages. It is also important that the objects within your web site are also kept together in a logical way.

2 Web Site Improvements

You might want to think of it like a shop or store. As a visitor to that store you expect to find all the DVDs in one place and all the books in another. Apply this to your web site and you will store all your PDF files neatly in one place, your audio clips in another and so on.

The web site structure or architecture that I have found to work extremely well on the internet is a four tier or a four level structure as shown in Figure 2.6. I have annotated this for the Cead-Books web site. Here are the salient facts for this web site:

- The theme for this site is **Mysteries**, more specifically **Ancient Mysteries** and even more specifically than that **Ancient Mysteries and Lost Worlds.** You can have a single word and hence a very narrow theme or something a bit wider - it doesn't really matter so long as the theme flows through the site. I found by experience that Mysteries by itself was just too wide.
- The objective of the web site is to get visitors intrigued by the range of mysteries and then get them to purchase recommended books via Amazon, thereby earning a commission payment, while letting Amazon do all the hard work.
- The only ancillary pages were called Home & Feedback, which left 6 pages to serve as the main information pages.

It is important to keep to your theme as if you deviate from it there is the risk that you add in all the items that appeal to you and then the only theme the site has is your personal preferences and not a definable topic.

Web Site Improvements 2

You will see later that I made that mistake in a slightly different way but it still had a detrimental effect on the web site. We have all made mistakes and there is nothing wrong with going through this stage as it may provide you with a much improved theme.

Important Note

At some point you may have to take your editor's red pen to your creation and weed out what is not part of your theme. This is a tough but necessary step.

Level	Cead Books	Comments
1	Introduction/Overview	This is the home page that introduces the customer to the purpose of the site. The theme of the site is **Ancient Mysteries.**
2	Individual history themes	The site then expands to cover **Ancient Mysteries from various parts of the world.**
3	Book listings	From each page the customer can then opt to visit the shop to choose books on **Ancient Mysteries** from this area of the world.
4	Individual book information and reviews	Here are the full details of the books together with other reviews. This level is provided by the affiliate book store.

Fig 2.6: A four-tier structure as applied to a real web site.

2 Web Site Improvements

This layout has one flaw in that the flow is from top to bottom. If I do nothing else it is possible that the search engines could miss my content entirely and end up on a third party web site.

The fact that your web site is recommending this other site will add to its ranking and not yours! You can use the internal links within a site as well as external links pointing into a site to modify the flow somewhat. Instead of linking directly to the third party I linked to an external page (outside the web page creation tool) within the same domain space and then out to the third party. This has the effect of holding a considerable amount of PageRank within the web site.

If I tell you that the objective of this web site was to make money by earning commission as a book store affiliate then I think that you will see that a balance had to be struck between getting a commission payment and creating a web site that attracted the visitor in the first place.

Ideally I wanted the search engines to index the pages at level 2 and maybe level 3 whilst not losing the site's ranking out to Amazon.

Step 1D - Keywords

I guess that you have come across the concept of keywords and how important they are in the world of search engines. Keywords are the words (also know as search terms) that an internet surfer enters into their browser to find web sites that have information corresponding to those particular words or combination of words (phrases). The user of the internet search engines work in this way and so the search engines themselves have decided to work in the same way.

Web Site Improvements 2

Fact 3: There is an important relationship between your content, theme and keywords and some very important rules that apply to them.

Keywords must reflect your theme.

&

You need to create your content around keywords.

&

'Keywords' can be single word keywords or multiple word keyword phrases.

You can work around the three elements of Theme, Content and Keywords in any order you like provided that you check the effect any change in one element is having on the other two.

Let me illustrate this point by a practical example. Say you start by having a theme of <u>Winter Flowering Bulbs</u>, pick some keywords like Crocus and Daffodils and then write a superb few pages on using bulbs for <u>all year</u> round colour in the garden.

The development of the content follows a natural or organic route but you have now drifted away from your theme and this needs to be corrected in some way or other.

2 Web Site Improvements

You now have a number of ways you can go:

- Expand your theme to 'All Year Round Bulbs' and add more keywords to reflect their use throughout the year. This will allow you to use your content to its fullest and give you a lot more options in the search engines.

- Stay with your original narrower theme and edit down your content.

- Decide that you will stay with the narrow theme and the articles covering the wider use of bulbs throughout the year as it fits in with your business objectives. The business may be very slack during the late autumn/early winter and the owner has time to operate a mail-order business whilst during the rest of the year there is only time to be out and about with customers. So if traffic to the site falls off in summer it is not too much of a problem.

The point that I am making is that all the best practice in the world may be at odds with business or other practical issues.

Important Note

If you have the time, don't be afraid to experiment with your web site and web pages. This is the best way to understand how search engines work.

Web Site Improvements 2

Ideal Site Structure

To optimise a site for the search engines it needs to be structured along certain logical lines. The search engine robots themselves are constructed using logic that is implemented in lines of code. You need to lay out the logic of your web site along similar thinking.

Level 1	Level 2	Level 3	Level 4
Topic 1 with Keyword A	Keyword A1	Keyword A1A	Keyword A1A1
			Keyword A1A2
		Keyword A1B	Keyword A1B1
			Keyword A1B2
	Keyword A2	Keyword A2A	Keyword A2A1
			Keyword A2A2
		Keyword A2B	Keyword A2B1
			Keyword A2B2

Fig 2.7: The keyword tree expands out into arms, branches and leaves.

Figure 2.7 has been simplified a bit to show how a single topic, probably the same as Keyword A, is expanded in the same way that a tree grows into arms, branches and leaves. The levels correspond to the number of words in the keyword phrase.

2 Web Site Improvements

Keyword Phrases	Best Position	Notes
Ancient Mysteries	Yahoo (UK) -10 Altavista (UK) -12 Overture (UK) -14 Looksmart -15	Also in Yahoo
Ancient History Egypt	Yahoo (UK) -44	
Lost Civilisations	Yahoo (UK) -15 Looksmart -19 Overture(UK) -19 Altavista(UK) -22	Also in AllTheWeb, Altavista, Yahoo
Israelites Sinai	Hotbot -9 Teoma -9 Ask Jeeves (UK) 11 Dogpile 13	
Noah Ark Ararat	Dogpile -20	
New Chronology		
Giza Pyramids Sphinx		
Shroud Turin		
Lost continent Mu		
Ancient astronauts		
Ark covenant		
Akenaten heretic pharaoh		

Fig 2.8: Summary of web site's performance in major search engines.

Web Site Improvements 2

Let's start with the site theme of Cead Books, which as you recall is all about (Ancient) Mysteries. Again the URL of this site is http://www.cead-books.co.uk. When I set the site up initially I used an SEO (Search Engine Optimization) tool to check on my rankings across the world and I was extremely disappointed by the results, which I have summarised in Figure 2.8.

Where there is no entry then the tool is basically saying that the site is not listed or is below the ranking threshold (50 in this case, which equals 5 pages of results) that I set. This is a less than ideal result but quite typical at this stage. Note the complete absence of entries for MSN and Google despite me notifying them of the existence of the web site.

Step 1E - Analysis

Even by stretching the relationships between the keywords and having a few more secondary ones thrown in, the result is not too pleasing. There are just too many blanks and that means that I am wasting opportunities and losing traffic and potential customers to my site.

Exercise 5

If you wish, you can now follow the steps that I went through and apply them to your own web site. If you do then I suggest that you take a blank sheet of paper and plot the keywords the way I have done in Figure 2.9.

This will quickly tell you the current health of your web site.

2 Web Site Improvements

Code KW	Level	Keyword	Keyword Type
A	Topic	Ancient Mysteries	T
A1	Level 2	Ancient History	A
A2	Level 2	Lost Civilisations	A
A1a	Level 3	Ancient History Egypt	B
A1b	Level 3	Ancient History Israel	B
A2a	Level 3	Lost Continent Mu	B
A2b	Level 3		B
A1a1	Level 4	Egypt: Giza Pyramids	L
A1a2	Level 4	Israel: Ark Covenant	L
A1b1	Level 4	Israel: Shroud of Turin	L
A1b2	Level 4	Egypt: Akenaten	L
A2a1	Level 4	New Chronology	L
A2a2	Level 4	Ancient Astronauts	L
A2b1	Level 4		L
A2b2	Level 4		L

Fig 2.9: The keywords plotted into the four-tier structure. The keywords are scattered and disjointed! See Figure 2.10 for Keyword Type.

Web Site Improvements 2

Code	Level	Type
T	Level 1 (tree)	Primary keyword comprising a single word
A	Level 2(arm)	Secondary keyword usually a phrase of 2 words but can be a single word.
B	Level 3 (branch)	Tertiary keyword usually of 2 to three words
L	Level 4 (leaf)	Long phrase of 3 or 4 words with an occasional 5 word phrase.

Fig 2.10: The Tree structure as a TABL acronym.

Step 1F - Learning Lessons

A lot of analysis had now been carried out on that web site but just what does it all mean and what had I learned as a result of this initial study? It is very important to be critical of your own work! Pretend to be a consultant analysing someone else's web site. You don't have to overdo it and do give praise for achievements so far.

Here is what I noted down from the preceding analysis:

1. I had achieved a success rate of about 42% with my 12 keyword phrases. That meant that just 5 of my keywords were being scored highly by any search engine. For the moment I was not about to tackle the other issue of my site not appearing in certain search engines. I made a mental note not to throw this minor success away by a radical redesign. See Chapter 6 for a review of free tools that will give you a ranking list from the search engines.

2 Web Site Improvements

2. A lot of my keywords were ancillary or inconsistent with my theme. This means that the web site is not flowing correctly and it is likely that the human viewer will find it a bit disjointed. It did look like that I had thrown the web site together even though I spent many hours on the content.

3. I was reaching into the UK pretty well and nowhere else. My second note to myself was to check if this was a feature of being a **.co.uk.**

4. My site was too spread out as I had tried to incorporate too many mysterious issues. Many of them now had no actual relationship to the theme as expanded by level 2. That content had to go!

In summary I could do a lot better and my plan was to redesign the site rather than tinker with it.

These are examples of the lessons that I learnt and I'm sure that you will have a slightly different list that will set your agenda. I would be surprised if you don't have a list of things to do but it could happen. If you are now in that happy position then read on and build on your success.

Important Note

Don't be afraid to tear a site down and implement a redesign. It may be the best option in the long run. It may actually be quicker than trying to tweak it or hoping that it will come good after next month's crawl by the robots. Do stand back a bit as you want to build on your successes to date and not to throw the baby out with the bath water either.

Web Site Improvements 2

Checklist 4

You should use this checklist in conjunction with Checklist Numbers 1 & 2.

- I need to reorganise my web pages using the four tier structure. (If your content only allows a two or three tier structure then work with that for the present.)

- I have to change the keyword phrases so that they both expand and flow down this multi-tier structure. The page content will have to match this.

- I will have to research new keywords to fill the gaps in the structure.

Step 2: Action Plan for Change

From the lessons learnt the next step is to evolve an action plan for each lesson learnt. This may produce one or more additional actions. You should already have a checklist of things to do and you should now combine everything into one big action plan that has both overall web site objectives and real actions combined together. If this has turned into a major undertaking you may want to plan out a programme of work so that you get the tasks in a logical sequence. The action of setting down a series of inter-related tasks will make you think about what has to be done and you will be surprised how many ideas will spring into your mind.

2 Web Site Improvements

At the very least I would recommend that you use 'to do' lists to force you to work in a disciplined way. If you just charge ahead you will make a mess of things!

Important Note

If the lesson you have learnt does not produce an action then question whether you have really learnt something!

My overall objectives looked like this:

1. I wanted a higher success rate for my keywords and I set my new target at 67%, which means that I wanted 8 of my 12 keyword phrases to appear in the search engines. I would need to spend a few days doing more **keyword research**. The next target would be 85% and then 100% - I don't expect to be able to achieve this all in one go. If I exceed a target at any particular stage then I will review the objectives set in the next stage

2. Prune any keywords that are not consistent with my theme. If you are like me then you probably threw in a few extra keywords just before you finally started submitting your site to the search engines! Time to get rid of them!

3. Consider making the site a .com or maybe a .biz to extend it beyond a national or regional boundary. Note that this is not a trivial step and that you may be introducing a redirect into your structure.

Web Site Improvements 2

4. I planned to redesign the site so that I had more control over the content at the lower tiers. Up to this point I had to accept the content provided by Amazon. If your site does not use a third party then the job can be somewhat easier.

5. I would have another look at Page Ranking and this would mean having a hard look at the links within the site and whether I was giving my ranking away to Amazon!

CEAD BOOKS-- Challenge Your N

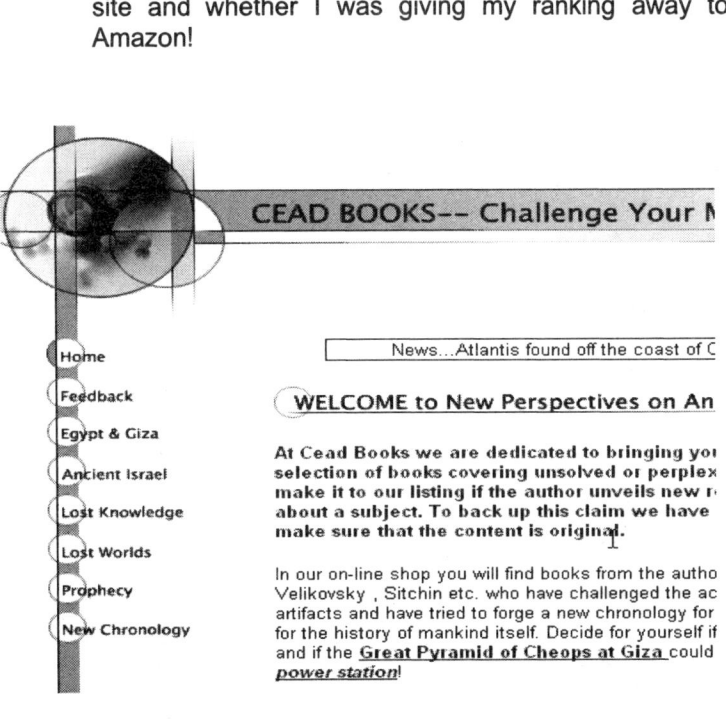

- Home
- Feedback
- Egypt & Giza
- Ancient Israel
- Lost Knowledge
- Lost Worlds
- Prophecy
- New Chronology

News...Atlantis found off the coast of C

WELCOME to New Perspectives on An

At Cead Books we are dedicated to bringing you selection of books covering unsolved or perplex make it to our listing if the author unveils new r about a subject. To back up this claim we have make sure that the content is original.

In our on-line shop you will find books from the autho Velikovsky, Sitchin etc. who have challenged the ac artifacts and have tried to forge a new chronology for for the history of mankind itself. Decide for yourself if and if the **Great Pyramid of Cheops at Giza** could *power station*!

Fig 2.11: Here is the original home page of Cead Books. Note the flat structure and how all of the pages are just one level below the top level (Home Page).

2 Web Site Improvements

This happened because I got totally bogged down in creating content to link to the e-commerce part of the site. I lost sight of the fact that if customers didn't find my web pages there was absolutely no way they could actually buy a product!

Step 2A - Keyword Research

In revisiting the problems with Cead-Books I came across a really useful tool to help with finding the keywords that surfers are using and this one is free to use. When I built the site for the first time I had used Wordtracker (http://www.wordtracker.com) and after a trial session paid to use it for a day to research some new keywords. To be honest I really wasn't sure what I had learned from all that analysis. Don't let me discourage you from paying the site a visit and deciding for yourself.

The other good site to have a look at is the Overture keyword suggestion tool.

Find it at:

http://inventory.overture.com/d/searchinventory/suggestion/

The really useful tool that I found is provided by Digital Point:

(http://www.digitalpoint.com/tools/suggestion).

This is a great **free** tool that links into both Wordtracker and Overture, the two primary routes to check what surfers are actually searching for. You need to create an account to get the full benefit but it will save you a lot of time in the long run.

Web Site Improvements 2

Phrase: Civilization
Market: United Kingdom   Only applies to Overture data
[Suggest]

Fig 2.12: The simple digitalpoint interface. Note that Overture only has data from certain countries.

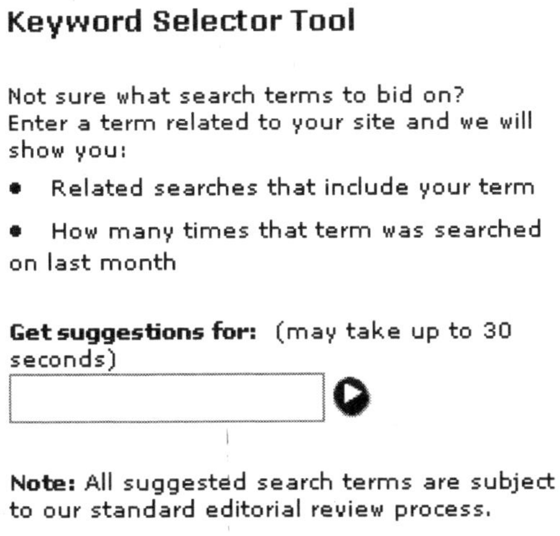

Keyword Selector Tool

Not sure what search terms to bid on?
Enter a term related to your site and we will show you:

- Related searches that include your term
- How many times that term was searched on last month

Get suggestions for: (may take up to 30 seconds)

Note: All suggested search terms are subject to our standard editorial review process.

Fig 2.13: the Overture Interface is very easy to use. Just enter your keyword or keywords to access the data.

2 Web Site Improvements

Get suggestions for: (may take up to 30 seconds)

ancient mysteries

Note: All suggested search terms are subject to our standard editorial review process.

Searches done in March 2006

Count	Search Term
1592	ancient mystery
128	mystery of ancient history
118	ancient domain of mystery
116	mystery of the ancient world
113	ancient aztalan indian mystery town
88	mystery of ancient egypt
83	ancient mystery schools
43	ancient mystery religion
34	mystery ancient ritual
29	ancient unsolved mystery

Fig 2.14: Results for the keyword search using the plural word 'mysteries' that has also returned the singular version.

Important Note

The data that you get back from the tools will differ somewhat due to the way it is gathered and processed.

Web Site Improvements 2

Overture does not differentiate between singulars and plurals but will consider 'civilisation' and 'civilization' as separate words. Using both American & British spellings as synonyms can provide a useful edge over web pages that only use one form of the spelling.

A search for both these words in Overture showed a count of 1528 for the former and a count of 11205 for the latter. Carry out a few searches using both tools to get a feel for the information they contain and how it is being interpreted.

Wordtracker	
Check out what else Wordtracker can do for you.	
aztec civilization	549.0 /day
mayan civilization	478.0 /day
ancient civilizations	455.0 /day
civilization 4	384.0 /day
civilization	335.0 /day
civilization iv	297.0 /day
inca civilization	249.0 /day
civilization 3	182.0 /day
olmec civilization	161.0 /day
civilization 3 cheats	148.0 /day
western civilization	137.0 /day
indus valley civilization	136.0 /day
ancient civilization	122.0 /day
maya civilization	116.0 /day
meaning of civilization	113.0 /day

Fig 2.15: Here are the results for 'civilization' from the digital point tool version of Wordtracker.

2 Web Site Improvements

Overture	
galactic civilization	64.5 /day
civilization	62.8 /day
civilization 4	32.1 /day
civilization iv	23.0 /day
galactic civilization 2	18.3 /day
civilization iii	14.5 /day
civilization galactic ii	14.0 /day
civilization game	13.0 /day
civilization 3	12.9 /day
ancient civilization	12.8 /day
clash of civilization	12.3 /day
civilization 3 game download	8.1 /day
civilization 2	6.8 /day
civilization board game	6.0 /day
civilization 3 cheat	5.3 /day
civilization call to power	4.4 /day
indus valley civilization	4.4 /day
galactic civilization ii dread lord	4.3 /day
civilization of china	3.9 /day
2 cheat civilization galactic	3.8 /day
civilization conquest	3.6 /day
civilization iv pc	3.0 /day
civilization sport	2.8 /day

Fig 2.16: The Overture data is very different to the Wordtracker information.

The more you use these two databases the more you will see how far apart their results can be. There is no simple explanation for this and the many answers in the various internet forums do not shed any real light on the matter.

Web Site Improvements 2

Wordtracker	
Check out what else Wordtracker can do for you.	
ancient mysteries	139.0/day
ancient machining mysteries	16.0/day
ancient earth mysteries	13.0/day
mystery cults of ancient greek religion	12.0/day
mysteries of ancient egypt	10.0/day
ancient mystery	9.0/day
ancient mysteries enigmas civilizations	8.0/day
ancient domains of mystery	6.0/day
unsolved ancient mystery	6.0/day
ancient mysteries enigmas underwater topography	5.0/day
mysteries of ancient history	5.0/day
mystery machine ancient	5.0/day
mystery of ancient american port	5.0/day
ancient mystery religions	4.0/day
ancient north american mysteries	4.0/day

Fig 2.17: Wordtracker results for 'ancient mysteries'.

I just use the data as a very rough guide as to the likely success of a particular keyword combination. The data changes over time so unless you can access the historical trends you don't know if this topic is becoming more or less popular.

As you look through these listings you will also spot keyword combinations that you did not even think about. I do advise that you type some of these keyword phrases into one of the search engines just to see what genre of web site they are going to return. Looking at Figures 2.15 and 2.16 indicates that a lot of the searches have been about computer games rather than an interest in history.

2 Web Site Improvements

Overture	
ancient mystery	3.9 /day
egypt ancient mystery	1.6 /day
ancient mystery world	0.6 /day
ancient great mystery seventy	0.5 /day
ancient cult mystery	0.4 /day
ancient culture hidden mystery	0.3 /day
ancient egypt fantasy murder mystery	0.3 /day
ancient job mystery	0.2 /day
ancient unsolved mystery	0.2 /day
ancient controversial knowledge mystery	0.2 /day
ancient egypt holding mystery over power	0.2 /day
mystery of ancient history	0.2 /day

Fig 2.18: The Overture data that only includes the singular form of the word.

Step 2B - Keyword Analysis

Having run all your keywords through these tools you are going to end up with a mass of data that needs co-ordinating in some way. And now here is what I have drawn up (Figure 2.19) for these and a few other words that fit into my slightly revised theme for Cead Books of the **Ancient Mysteries** left by **Lost Civilizations**.

Ancient Mysteries of Lost Civilisations			
Ancient Mysteries		New Chronology	Lost Civilisations	
Prehistory	Biblical		Ancient	Pre-flood

Fig 2.19: I decided to fit the keywords into this structure.

Web Site Improvements 2

This structure takes up eight pages and I can link out to third party web sites from all levels. Linking between the pages will improve the PageRank of each one. If you refer back to the Cead Books graphic in Figure 2.11 you will see that the pages on Prophecy, Lost Knowledge and Feedback have been removed. Others will be incorporated under new headings. I will provide a mechanism for Customer feedback in some other way that doesn't take up a whole page.

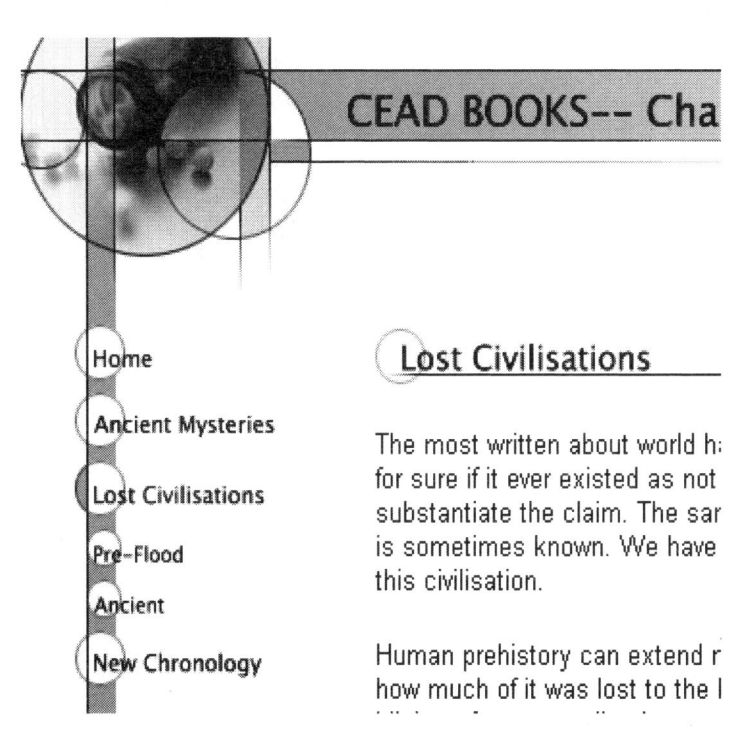

Fig 2.20: Here is the revised Cead Books front page that mirrors the keyword driven structure in Figure 2.19.

81

2 Web Site Improvements

Step 2C - Keyword Refinement

The next stage is to tabulate all that keyword data and see if it makes any sense! Don't be surprised if you get conflicting information!

<u>Ideally you want keyword phrases that lots of people use to search on but are not used as keywords by our competing sites</u>

I think you and I both know that this is just not going to happen very often given the size of the Internet and the fact that a lot of people are aware of the basics of how to use keywords. There are some tools around but they really just serve to confuse the issue. There is a measure called the Keyword Effectiveness Index (KEI) and you can calculate this number yourself quite easily.

$$KEI = DS^2/C$$

DS = Daily World Searches and C = the number of web sites returned by using a keyword search tool.

For example if DS = 335 per day and Google returns 99.4 million pages for that keyword search then the KEI for that word is just 0.001. The designer of the KEI recommends a KEI of at least 10 and ideally around 100 for the keyword to be really effective. It just doesn't happen any more!

This measure is not widely used as it makes no allowance for the quality of the competition and it is not very scientific due to the way the Daily World Searches are derived. One school of thought says that you only really have to worry about 20 web sites as they are the ones keeping you out of the coveted positions in the ranking! It is a thought worth remembering.

Web Site Improvements 2

Here are a few other ideas that might give you some competitive advantage:

- Misspellings – many people misspell common words and in your particular market may be very common. You can try to include them along with the correct spellings at strategic points in your pages in the keyword META tag and in the first paragraph. As you will see in a later chapter this may not be a good idea

- Mixing in both UK and US spellings. Consider also Canadian & Australian variations.

- Typing errors such as running words together, missing out a hyphen or an apostrophe.

I have never really bought into the misspelling argument as it only happens for a small percentage of the time. It is worth checking the statistics on your web site if it provides this information or via Google as there may quite frequent misspellings that could be quite useful to know about.

Step 2D - Applying the Keyword Research

I decided to plot my keyword choices into a matrix (see Figure 2.21) so that I could quickly evaluate my progress and check for any serious omissions.

Note that not every possible part of the matrix has been filled. The research has turned up new words like 'prehistory', 'timeline' and 'antiquity'. These are valuable words that may be synonyms of your primary keywords so do note them for possible inclusion in your content.

2 Web Site Improvements

Single Word	2 word	3 word	4 word
Chronology	Bible Chronology, Biblical Chronology, Egyptian Chronology	Chronology of the Old Testament	
Civilization	Ancient Civilizations		
Ancient	Ancient Egypt, Ancient India Ancient history Ancient Civilizations	Mysteries Ancient Egypt, Ancient History Mystery	
Prehistory	Prehistory Timeline, Antiquity Prehistory, Human Prehistory	Old World Prehistory, Ice Age prehistory	
Atlantis		Lost City Atlantis Lost Empire Atlantis	
Lemuria	Atlantis Lemuria		Lost Continent Mu Lemuria
Israel	Ancient Israel	Twelve tribes Israel	
	History Israel		
Mysteries	Ancient Mysteries	Mysteries Ancient World	

Fig 2.21: Keywords tabulated into 2, 3 & 4 word phrases that will then be translated into the four tier structure. This can be found in Appendix 1.

Web Site Improvements 2

Exercise 6

You should now work with the keyword suggestion tools to create your own matrix of keyword phrases just as I have done with my own web site. Put a threshold in of something like 5 searches per day below which you won't use that keyword.

- *Continue to use keywords that are working well. For example Lost Civilisations and Ancient Mysteries in the example.*

- *Identify new keyword phrases using the structure in Figure 2.19 as the starting point – prehistory was something that I never thought about in the early stages of the web site's development.*

- *Modify existing phrases: a good example is to change the phrase 'Ancient History Egypt' to 'Mysteries Ancient Egypt'.*

- *Build up your results into a similar matrix to Figure 2.21, ideally filling in each square. Don't worry if some squares remain blank.*

Exercise 7

Transfer your new set of keywords into a matrix shown in Appendix 1 to see if they fit together in two ways:

- *First of all they have to match the theme of the site.*

2 Web Site Improvements

- *If one or two are doubtful and you don't really want to get rid of them then it won't do much harm to hang onto them for the moment. Your next site review will convince you one way or the other!.*

- *Secondly they need to cascade down the tiers in a consistent way.*

- *One or two out of kilter phrases may still be present and they can be refined next time around. Equally there may be a few blanks and you will just have to live with that.*

I have reproduced the final version in Appendix 1. The new matrix now looks a lot better than the first attempt. However, it will have to be tested out for real and you will only know how successful the work has been once the robots have visited again.

Do note that it may not be possible on this or any iteration to fill in every keyword position without 'distorting' the readability of the site too much.

More work can be done between now and the next iteration but the important thing is to get the new version up onto your web site so that the search engines can index it.

Web Site Improvements **2**

Step 3 - Making the Changes

By now you have gathered up a lot of changes that need to be applied to your web site. In addition to the items from the various checklists you should have:

- A revised web site structure.
- A revised set of web page layouts and page titles.
- A new set of keywords.
- Newly edited content to be distributed across the web pages.

Now that the keywords have been identified it is time to edit the content. At the very least you will have to move some pages around and transfer content between pages. However it is time to check another concept out that is called **Keyword Density**.

Opinion is currently divided on how important this really is as the search engines are now wise to the various techniques that have been used in the past to affect this measure.

One school of thought says that if you have **themed and** then **structured** your site correctly then don't worry about keyword density.

The search engines are very wise to a technique called 'keyword stuffing' where the most strategic parts of the web site are just jammed full with your keywords. Google and the others are wise to this and may even ban your site if they determine that you are an offender.

2 Web Site Improvements

As I have mentioned Keyword Density the best advice that I can give you is that it should be somewhere between 1 & 2% at the very least. That means that a keyword needs to be included for every fifty words you write about your topic. This would ensure that you meet this target. Don't forget that synonyms do count in this total.

However you don't want to write rubbish just to meet a target. Write naturally and enthusiastically about your topics and you will easily meet the targets.

Internal PageRank

Exercise 8

Take a blank sheet of paper and draw out your site with a square for each page and then draw in the internal links and any external links from your site to sites that you are recommending or think are important.

Keep the drawing safe as we will use it in a few minutes.

PageRank is a fairly simple concept although the method of calculating it is complex as it takes many iterative calculations. The underlying theory says that if Page 1 links to Page 2 then Page 1 is saying that Page 2 is an important page. Also if Page 2 has more important links to it than other pages then this is also saying that Page 2 is an important page. PageRank also gets distributed across pages.

Web Site Improvements 2

The important things to do are:

- Get links from appropriate sites that are of good quality. By appropriate I mean relevant to your site with content and a theme similar to your own web site.

- You want to keep PageRank within your site by linking out from pages that have a low PageRank and a lot of internal links.

- If you do have a links page then instead of linking directly out make that page 'sticky' by linking to a page within your site before linking out to the third party. If I use this method I turn this intermediate page into a links review page by adding a personal view of the third party web sites. Finish off by putting links back to the most important pages on your own web site. The overall effect is to keep a large proportion of the PageRank score within your web site.

- Make sure that any links page (site map) has less than 25 links on it to avoid the spiders thinking that it is just a link farm trying to artificially boost a web site's ranking.

- Gets your web site listed in expert or niche directories.

Meta Tags

Having gone through the visible part of your web site you now must double check the invisible area such as the various HTML tags. The source code captured from the Radio Engineering web site is shown in Figure 2.22.

2 Web Site Improvements

```
<!DOCTYPE HTML PUBLIC "-//W3C//DTD HTML 4.0 Transitional//EN">
<HTML>
<HEAD>
<TITLE>Digital Radio Technology</TITLE>
<META HTTP-EQUIV="Content-Type" CONTENT="text/html; charset=ISO-8
<META NAME="Author" CONTENT="Kevin Ryan">
<META NAME="Abstract" CONTENT="Educating hobbyists, enthusiasts a
<META NAME="Copyright" CONTENT="KPR i-Services Limited">
<META NAME="contact_addr" CONTENT="PO Box 2430 Reading RG4 8WW">
<META NAME="Description" CONTENT="Educating hobbyists, enthusiast
<META NAME="Date" CONTENT="$date">
<META NAME="Keywords" CONTENT="Digital Radio Technology ,Digital
<META NAME="Generator" CONTENT="NetObjects Fusion 8 for windows">
<META NAME="Robots" CONTENT="ALL">
<LINK REL=STYLESHEET TYPE="text/css" HREF="./style.css">
<LINK REL=STYLESHEET TYPE="text/css" HREF="./site.css">
<STYLE>
</STYLE>
</HEAD>
<BODY NOF="(MB=(ZeroMargins, 146, 433, 136, 27), L=(HomeLayout, 7
    <TABLE CELLPADDING=0 CELLSPACING=0 BORDER=0 WIDTH=880 NOF=LY)
        <TR VALIGN=TOP ALIGN=LEFT>
```

Fig 2.22: Source code showing many of the META tags.

There are two categories of META tags. The first is the HTTP-EQUIV type that simulates the HTTP commands to the web server. HTTP is the Hyper Text Transfer Protocol that defines how a web server and a browser communicate with each other. There are a handful of commands that can be useful for a web site owner. Some of them are generated automatically by a programme such as Net Objects Fusion.

The second type is the NAME attributes that are read by search engines. I cover the important NAME tags later in this chapter and in chapter 5.

Web Site Improvements 2

META HTTP TAGS

The syntax is as follows:

<META HTTP-EQUIV = "type" CONTENT="parameters">

Code examples:

<META HTTP-EQUIV="expires" CONTENT="Mon 26 Aug 2006 00:01:01 GMT">

<META HTTP-EQUIV="pragma" CONTENT="no cache">

<META HTTP-EQUIV="Refresh" CONTENT="60;URL=http://www.one.co.uk">

<META HTTP-EQUIV="set cookie" CONTENT="cookievalue=mycook; expires=Mar 21 2007 00:01:01 ;path=/cookies">

<META HTTP-EQUIV="Content-type" CONTENT="text/html; charset=ISO-8859-1">

The main tags are listed in Figure 2.23. You will use this information just now and again but it may just save you some time tracking down some unusual or unexplained behaviour on the part of a search engine. More often than not you just won't have any problems with these HTTP tags as they are passed transparently between the web server and the browsers.

2 Web Site Improvements

Type	Parameters	Function
expires	date and time	Can be used to keep content current by letting files have a shelf life. However, only the Netscape browser seems to use this tag.
pragma	no cache	Tells the browser not to cache (keep a local copy) the page so that a new copy is downloaded every time.
refresh	delay in seconds and optionally a new URL to load	Useful to display a short message and redirect the user to another site.
Set cookie	Cookie name and expiry date of cookie	Stores a cookie on the user's PC that expires on a particular date.
Content-type	Text/Html and a character set	Used to overcome any display problems.

Fig 2.23: The main types of HTTP META tags. This is just for reference.

META NAME TAGS

The NAME tags all follow this format:

<META NAME="tag name" CONTENT="attributes">

There are two very important name tags that are used by a number of the search engines.

Web Site Improvements 2

TITLE tag

You should create a unique and meaningful title for each of your web pages. The title shows up in the web browser and you should make sure that it is rich in keywords – it doesn't have to be a proper sentence as you will usually want to remove any common words.

If you have a site of some 30 pages tightly focused on a topic then this is not easy. However you don't want a page to be listed in the search engine as 'UNTITLED' so spend some time working on variations to the main titles.

If you can, place those keywords that occur most frequently on a particular page into your web page titles.

DESCRIPTION tag

Many search engines (I believe that this only applies to Google and its feeder search engines) are now reckoned not to use this any more but I always make sure that there is something meaningful in the tag.

Yahoo recommends that your site includes a description META tag that is written accurately and carefully. As with the TITLE tag, the DESCRIPTION tag should fit in the content of the site.

Altavista (see Figure 2.25) also picked up some meaningful information from the META content in the header. So don't be too quick in discarding the DESCRIPTION tag as a useful way of influencing the search engines as not all of them follow the Google model.

2 Web Site Improvements

Web Results
Page 1 of 292 results containing **site:www.radioeng.co.uk** (0.11 seconds)

Register. UK Domain Names - www.tv
The Official Site to Register. UK Domain Names.

Digital Radio Technology
Educating hobbyists, enthusiasts and technophiles about digital radio technology. Digital Radio now forum covers most forms of digital radio technology ...
www.radioeng.co.uk Cached page

Fig 2.24: Here is what MSN displays about the Radio Engineering web site. This is slightly different to Altavista.

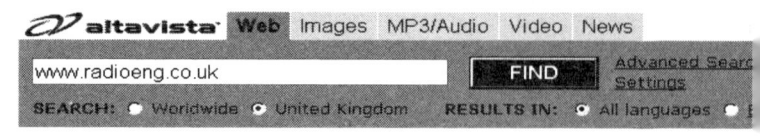

AltaVista found 299 results

Digital Radio Technology
Educating hobbyists, enthusiasts and technophiles about digital radio technology. bands : Digital Radio Mondiale and IBOC for the AM Bands , IBOC and Digital Au bands and there is also ...
www.radioeng.co.uk
More pages from radioeng.co.uk

Fig 2.25: Altavista has picked up information from both the Title & Description tags.

ROBOTS tag

This is dealt with elsewhere in some detail. It is worth noting that Altavista has defined two additional attributes of noimageindex and noimageclick

Code examples:
<META NAME="description" CONTENT="A short description of my web site">

Web Site Improvements 2

This brings you to the end of quite an extensive overhaul of your web site. You have now created a web site and a set of web pages that will be noticed by the search engines.

This is enough work for you to complete at the moment as the new web pages now need to be submitted to the search engines to see what they make of all the changes.

Checklist 5

Here is a final high level checklist to make sure that you have checked and changed whatever you can:

- The web site has a theme that binds all the individual pages together.

- The site structure is per the 4-tier model with good navigation between pages.

- The web site has a minimum of 6 content or information pages and each page has several hundred words of naturally written content.

- The keywords flow and expand through the site with 1 to 3 keyword phrases per page.

- The META tags contain precise and concise information.

- There is a site map with one link from the home page.

2 Web Site Improvements

Summary

This chapter was aimed at rescuing an existing web site and transforming it into a good quality web site. You can, of course, apply all these tips and techniques to a brand new web site.

If you are starting from scratch, then begin with a theme and from that theme develop a set of topics and sub-topics that expand on the theme and also map onto a structured set of web pages.

Next you need to research single keywords plus their synonyms and keyword phrases that reinforce the theme and topics and map these onto the structured web pages as well. The keywords and topics may or may not be the same but they must be related to each other.

Now that you have the basic framework you can start creating your content, making sure that you are well within the recommendations in this chapter. Try to get the web pages to overlap each other in content.

All this work should help you decide on the domain name of the web site and the URL names and titles of the pages. Try to avoid all the common mistakes listed at the start of this chapter and put in a good navigation structure and site map.

Next Chapter

The next chapter will tell you how to submit your web site to the major search engines and a selection of search directories. I strongly recommend using a manual process rather than automatic submission software.

3. Search Engine Submission

It may seem obvious but before you go any further you must now load the new web pages and keywords that you have created up onto your web server. Once the pages have been uploaded via FTP you should carry out some extensive checking of the web site and create an error log of the problems that you find. It is very important that you follow all your links via a browser to the internal pages as this is exactly what the search engine robot will do.

It is very easy to have moved your web pages around and have forgotten to check every link, especially if you have created pages outside of a graphical web site creation package. If the error log is long then you may decide that your pages need a lot more work. You can do much of this work offline but at some point you have to test your web site for real by loading it onto its final home. Once you have pushed your web site across that minimum threshold of acceptability it is time to submit it or re-submit it to a selection of search engines and directories. You should have selected a handful of directories as part of your research in chapter 2.

Manual URL Submission

The major search engines such as Google, Yahoo, ASK and MSN claim that they now find most new web sites automatically and this is generally true. ASK does not provide a 'submit URL' facility and prefers to find new web sites by following HREF links from existing sites. This discovery process happens in and around the end of each calendar month.

3 Search Engine Submission

Checklist 6

- Submit my web site manually to Google.
- Submit my web site manually to Yahoo.
- Submit my web site manually to MSN.
- Submit my web site manually to at least three general or global directories.
- Submit my web site manually to at least one specialist directory.
- Submit my web site manually to DMOZ.
- I will monitor progress every month after the search engines have updated their indexes.

To help you tick off the actions on this checklist I will now show you how to complete each of these tasks. Web sites can be submitted manually, semi-automatically or automatically. I favour either of the first two as it gives you control over the process and you can act on any error messages that might appear. Many of the search engines now require the input of a visual confirmation code to identify if an automatic process has been used to submit a URL. Don't be worried about companies offering to submit your URL to 1000's of search engines - less than 10 really matter!

Search Engine Submission 3

Manual submission is where you enter the details of your web site on a submission page. The major search engines usually just require you to enter the full URL of the domain (http://www.mydomain.co.uk) but the search engine directories do require a lot more detail.

Many of the big players claim that they pick up the majority of new sites automatically and this does seem to be true. I have found automatic submission to be a bit of a lottery so I now submit my sites by hand to just three search engines.

Google

Google doesn't make it easy for you to add your URL. I have trawled around their help pages so often that I now find it by typing in a search of '**submit URL Google**' into the Google search engine.

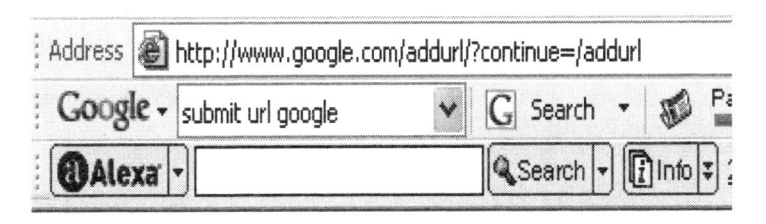

Fig 3.1: Finding the Google URL submission page.

3 Search Engine Submission

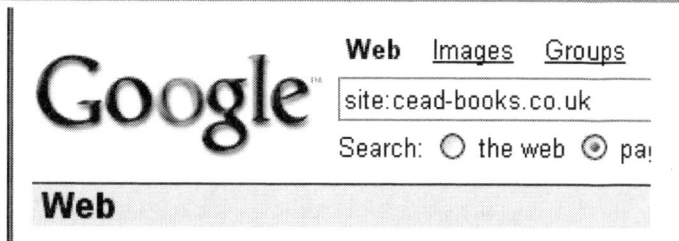

> Web   Images   Groups
>
> **Google** site:cead-books.co.uk
>
> Search: ○ the web ● pa
>
> **Web**
>
> Ancient Mysteries History Civilisations
> Books on the ancient mysteries of lost civilisations and world history.
> www.cead-books.co.uk/ - 15k - Cached - Similar pages

Fig 3.2: By entering the 'site' command you can find if Google already knows about your web site.

As you explore this area of Google do note the 'Webmaster Info' link that takes you to www.google.com/webmasters where there is a lot of information on how Google indexes web sites. It does provide loads of advice on what to do and on what might be causing Google to ignore your site. It is worth reading for background information.

> **My site and Google**
> - Webmaster guidelines
> - My site in the Google index
> - Removals
> - Googlebot
> - Feedfetcher
> - More

Fig 3.3: Google's extensive help for webmasters

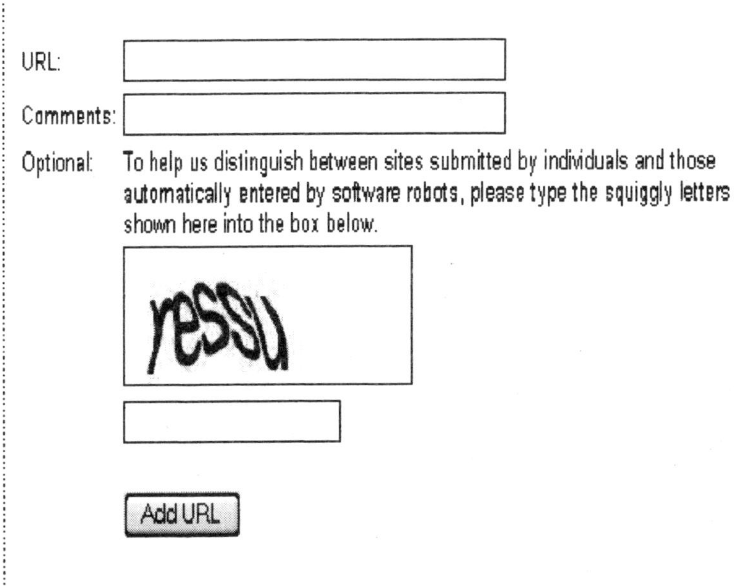

Search Engine Submission 3

URL:	[ ]
Comments:	[ ]

Optional: To help us distinguish between sites submitted by individuals and those automatically entered by software robots, please type the squiggly letters shown here into the box below.

[ressu]

[   ]

[Add URL]

Fig 3.4: Google like many sites want to make sure that a human is making the submission

On the same page Google then invites you to submit just the top level URL of your site. The Googlebot or the Google robot will then follow the links on your web site to find all the web pages. The second thing to note is that to prevent this page being used by bulk loaders or other frowned on submission practices you are required to read some squiggly letters to prove that a real person is actually submitting the site. Just enter the required information and click the add URL button and the job is done.

3 Search Engine Submission

Google Information for Webmasters

Thank you

Your URL has been successfully added.

Fig 3.5: The Google acknowledgement that the URL has been added to the crawl list.

Webmaster Help Center

Help Center Home

Google Sitemaps Home

Documentation
About Google Sitemaps
Sitemap Generator
Sitemap Protocol

Tools

My site and Google

- Webmaster guidelines
- My site in the Google index
- Removals
- Googlebot
- Feedfetcher
- More

Fig 3.6: Read the section about getting your site listed on Google – it is worth the time and effort.

Search Engine Submission 3

There is one area of Google that I must draw your attention to and that is the section on removing some or all of your web site from various parts of the Google system. **Proceed with caution at all times and read every word carefully.** Some of the options appear innocuous but can be very dangerous. Consider the warning buried away in Figure 3.9 where your complete URL could be suspended for a long time.

Please select an option below for instructions. Removals will take effect the next time Google crawls your site.

- Remove your entire website
- Remove part of your website
- Remove snippets
- Remove cached pages
- Remove an outdated link
- Remove an image from Google Image Search
- Remove a blog from Blog Search
- Remove a RSS or Atom feed (i.e., block Feedfetcher)
- Remove transcoded pages

Fig 3.7: Google provides detailed instructions on how to remove some or all of your web site

Quite sensibly Google has put some security around the facilities to prevent abuse of this very powerful set of tools. First of all you need to create an account to access this control console.

Google is consolidating all its systems into one giant portal so this account will prove useful for all the other Google-only things such as sitemaps, Adwords and so on

3 Search Engine Submission

First time here?

In order to remove a URL from the Google index, we need to first verify your e-mail address. Please enter it below, along with a password.

Email:
Password:
Confirm Password:

[Create Account]

Fig 3.8: The Google Remove URL screen.

The Google tools are very powerful and if you want to explore their features then I would suggest that you practise on a test web site. If you don't want to incur the extra expense of a second web hosting account then I would recommend that you avoid these utilities. If you do decide to experiment with a second web site then be careful about bringing up an exact copy of your web pages on a similar sounding URL as Google may see this as a mirror site. Site mirroring is yet another practice that is frowned upon as being open to abuse by spammers. A search engine spammer is someone who wants to deceive a search engine into providing their web pages with an artificially high, undeserved ranking.

Google™ — Remove your URL

Options

You may process your URL for removal from Google's search results. URLs will be removed after we've verified your request. Bear in mind that verification can take several days or longer and all pages submitted via the automatic URL removal system will be removed from the Google index temporarily for six months. You may review the status of submitted requests in the column to the right. To remove your Usenet posts from Google Groups, please click here.

Select only one:

- **Remove pages, subdirectories or images using a robots.txt file.**
  Your robots.txt file need not be in the root directory.

- **Remove a single page using meta tags.**

- **Remove an outdated link.**

Fig 3.9: Be warned about removing a URL in a moment of frustration!

If you want to remove pages and images from the Google index then I recommend that you use the robots.txt file to achieve your objectives. It will take 2 or 3 months for the process to work right through but it is much safer than wading in with these heavyweight Google tools. Once you have a Google account you will be able to see the actions the Googlebot has taken on your web site.

3 Search Engine Submission

Status

2005-07-18 12:56:31 GMT :
removal of image http://www.2ndbiz.co.uk/Paypal1/ *expired*

2005-07-18 12:56:31 GMT :
removal of http://www.2ndbiz.co.uk/Paypal1/ *expired*

2005-07-18 12:56:31 GMT :

Fig 3.10: Google's record of changes in the robots.txt file.

MSN

Fig 3.11: I have found MSN to be much quicker off the mark than any other search engine in finding web sites.

Search Engine Submission 3

The page to submit a URL is hard to find in MSN as well. Use the same technique of entering a search query to find where the page has shifted to. MSN are currently updating the whole search system so it may have moved to another location. Note that MSN, like Google, favours manual submission over automatic.

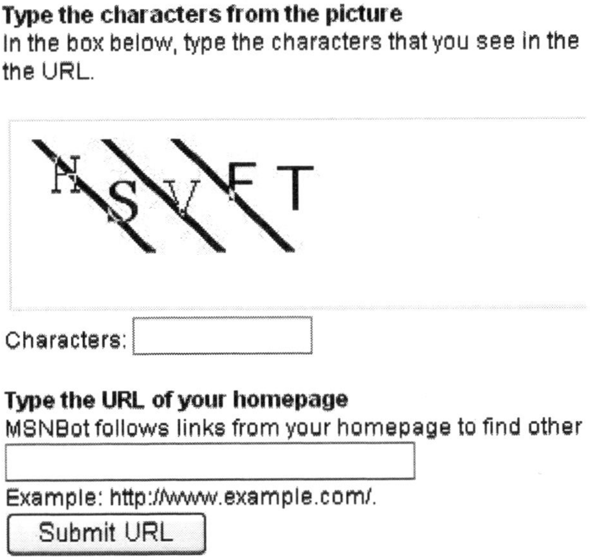

Type the characters from the picture
In the box below, type the characters that you see in the the URL.

Characters: [   ]

Type the URL of your homepage
MSNBot follows links from your homepage to find other
[   ]
Example: http://www.example.com/.
[Submit URL]

Fig 3.12: The MSN web page to submit your web site by hand.

The submission process should be straightforward and simple. If you have any problems then immediately submit your web site again as MSN should be able to see from their error logs that a genuine problem occurred.

3 Search Engine Submission

MSN Search Web Crawler and Site Indexing

- About site indexing on MSN Search
- Guidelines for successful indexing
- About site ranking
- About your site description
- Control which pages of your website are indexed
- Block your website from MSN Search Preview
- Troubleshoot issues with MSNBot and site crawling
- What to do when your site moves
- Remove your website from the MSN Search index

Fig 3.13: MSN provides similar information to Google but not as many tools and facilities. Like Google it is worth digesting what MSN has to say and apply it where appropriate.

While you are browsing the MSN site do have a look at the Sandbox section where MSN tells you about their latest ideas to make the web more relevant to users.

MSN has a growing network of search systems and you may get a very different view depending on how you click through their network. For example if your starting point is http://www.msn.com, a local search will probably take you to http://uk.msn.com. I have found that the best starting point for the UK is from http://search.msn.co.uk.

Note that MSN is piloting a local search facility where you set your home town and that really narrows down your search results. If your web site is aimed locally then make sure that you modify your descriptions, page titles and keywords accordingly.

Search Engine Submission 3

Yahoo

Yahoo! International		» See all
Aus & NZ	France	India
Canada	Germany	Italy

How to Suggest a Site | Company Info | Privacy P
Copyright © 2006 Yahoo! UK. All rights reserved.

Fig 3.14: Yahoo welcomes new web sites.

Happily Yahoo is bit more user friendly and down at the bottom of the page is a link (How to Suggest a Site) to URL submission. However you do need to acquire a User ID and Password, which is straightforward.

YAHOO! search
UK & IRELAND

Search > Help

Search Basics
How Yahoo! Search works

Fig 3.15: Yahoo has good help pages but has little in the way of innovative tools.

3 Search Engine Submission

YAHOO! SEARCH

Welcome to Yahoo! Search

Sign in with your ID

New to Yahoo!?
Sign up now to enjoy Yahoo! Search

- Sign in or sign up to customise Yahoo! Search.
- Make the same settings available at home or at work or on any computer you use, just by signing in!
- See local information in your search results (like best fares for your holiday searches).

Fig 3.16: You need a Yahoo account to submit your URL.

Enter the URL for your feed: http://

You can also submit a single webpage for inclusion.

Enter the URL for your page: http://www.radio-digital.co.uk

For any URL (directly submitted or obtained from a feed) our crawler already. We will automatically detect updates on pages and remove

Fig 3.17: You just need to enter the domain name to get Yahoo to pick up all the pages.

Search Engine Submission 3

Search Engine Directories

The next thing to do is to register your site with a few of what are called 'Minor Search Engine Directories', where we are pretty sure that Google and MSN are going to stop by and pick up the information. These directories fall into both the Free and Paid for Categories.

Ideally you want the web site to be in the Open Directory (DMOZ) and Yahoo but the former is so slow and the latter too expensive for most people. DMOZ is now taking many months to get round to reviewing your site and we just don't want to wait that long. We will register with DMOZ and just leave it at that for the next couple of months.

Name	URL	Cost	Comments
Worldsite Index	www.worldsiteindex.com	Free	Just 2 days to get listed
SearchSight	www.searchsite.com	Free	Just 2 days to get listed.
Linkopedia	www.linkopedia.com	£5.50	A modest cost and a very quick response usually next day.

Fig 3.18: List of search directories that work.

The plan is to register your web site with 2 or 3 free directories and 1 or 2 paid for ones. The aim is to keep the costs down. These are just for starters as you can consider other options depending on the success of stage one of the campaign.

3 Search Engine Submission

Why Do I Need To Bother With This?

The simple answer is most of the search engines use incoming links as a way of evaluating a web site. If nobody is linking to you then the reasoning is that your site must not be very relevant to the online community! Agree with it or not but that is the way it works!

How Do I Register With A Minor Search Engine?

This is usually a very easy process. In fact the hardest part is going to be choosing a category and/or a subcategory for your listing. The bigger the site the more difficult this is. With almost all of these directories you can submit your URL from any point within the Directory.

TIP :
Do a final check on your site to ensure that everything on the web site works OK and that the links are all in good order. I have had a site rejected due to broken links.

The generic process is as follows:

1. Go to the web site address or URL for the directory – www.searchsight.com is a good example.

2. Go to the Directory itself if you find that you are on a promotional page.

3. Check that you are not listed already – rare but it can happen!

Search Engine Submission 3

4. Start browsing the categories to find the best match for your website. Sometimes you will just have to settle for the best fit. Some Directories offer you the chance to suggest a new category but this will likely double the time for the submission.

5. Once you have found the spot then click on 'submit your site/URL' and you should find yourself on a screen similar to this one from Searchsight shown in Figure 3.19.

After your web page is evaluated, you will receive an email which will contain your web page listing information. If your web page is already in our listings, it will be scheduled to be re-evaluated. To check if your web page is already listed, you may go to the listing search page. Entering comments is optional. Category, country, and postal information is optional as well, though only listings that contain this information can be included in our directory. You may also go to the Listing Manager to edit your listing categories.

Please note: We are seeing an increase of URL's that are being submitted under irrelevant categories and countries. If we find URL's submitted with improper information, we will remove all listings that you have submitted, even if the other listings have correct information. Please only submit your URL's with accurate information.

Also note: SearchSight.com only accepts submissions that are suitable for viewing by all ages (no adult sites). SearchSight.com does not list all web pages submitted to us. Please consult our Terms of Service and our Help/FAQ's with any questions.

Category: (optional)	Radio / Audio	view entire list
ZIP/Postal Code: (optional)		what's this?
Country: (optional)	United Kingdom	
Comments: (optional)		
Web Site URL:	http://www.radioeng.co.uk	
Email Address:		

Fig 3.19: Searchsight information page. Do read the instructions carefully.

3 Search Engine Submission

World Site Index

Home
New Sites
Contact Us
Add Site
Link to Us

Directory / Shopping & Services / Books / History

Site Submission

We have filled the form below, using information from your website, please check and complete the form to continue.

Email Address: kryan@kpr-i-services.co.uk
This is needed to send you a confirmation email.
(NOTE: Not shown on site)

Site Title: Ancient Mysteries History Civilisations
Business name or the official title of your site (100 characters max).

- Must be in English.
- Do not use this field for keywords.
- Do not use ALL CAPITAL letters.
- Do not use prices, contact information, any time sensitive information etc.

Keywords: Ancient Mysteries, Ancient History of Egypt,
A list of keywords up to 200 characters long. Separate each keyword with a comma and space.

URL: http://www.cead-books.co.uk

Enter a Password:
Password used to modify your listing. Do not use a password that can be easily guessed. Must be more than 6 characters long.

Express submissions may include an additional 5 links to sub pages of the site; **any links not meeting the following requirements will be removed**:

- The link **must** point to a page that is part of your site and which can be accessed from the home page.
  If the route from the home page isn't immediately obvious then include directions in the comment field below.
- The link **must not** point to a page which has a limited lifespan, e.g. a promotional offer.
- The domain for the links **must** match that of the site being submitted.
- The link title **must** be representative of the page content and each title **must** be different.
- Each page **must** have different content.

Fig 3.20: World Site Index information pages. Again read them carefully.

114

Search Engine Submission 3

Other sites capture the relevant data from your own site. A good check that everything is in order! The screenshots from Worldsiteindex illustrate the point. It is all very straightforward provided you take it a step at a time.

For the sites that require payment you will need a credit card or a PayPal account to get your listing. Linkopedia works well with PayPal and you shouldn't have any problem. You can use any credit card with PayPal and you don't have to sign up for a PayPal account. You just need to follow the link for people who don't have a PayPal account. Linkopedia works in US dollars so it can work out as good value for money as it is regarded as one of the expert directories.

Pay special attention to the lower part of screen as shown in Figure 3.22 as that gives you a real idea as to how concise you need to be with your listing. Take some time with this as it is the most important start that you can give your website.

A Listing in Linkopedia Includes the Following Features:

- Get listed in 24 hours. Submitted listings are added to database within 24 to 48 hours subject to the submission terms & conditions being met.
- Featured in the **"What's New"** section of Linkopedia.
- **Permanent Listing.** Submitted listings never expire from the database.
- **Automatic Notification upon acceptance and entry.**
- **Quick and easy submission.**

RATE: One Time Payment $9.95 - per URL submitted.

Fig 3.21: The main advantage of using Linkopedia is that you get a permanent listing.

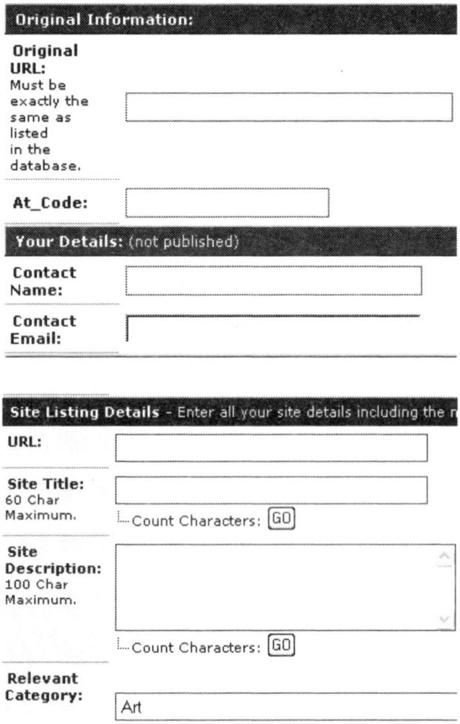

3 Search Engine Submission

Fig 3.22: The main screens in Linkopedia. Note the strict character limits of 60 for the title and just 100 for the description.

Does it Work?

Let me tell you of a quick way to check it out. In addition to the 'site' command there is another one called 'link'. So to check out the effectiveness of these minor directory engines I typed some commands into MSN and Google to find out.

Search Engine Submission 3

The command is: **link:www.domainname.com**

```
Web  News  Images  Desktop  Encarta
link:www.radioeng.co.uk                    [ Search ]
+Search Builder   Settings   Help   Español
```

Web Results
1-10 of 21 containing **link:www.radioeng.co.uk** (0.30 seconds)

Linkopedia. : Reference/Education/Distance Learning
Home : Reference : Education : Distance Learning Search by Keyword(s)   Subm
Listings: CoursePal Online degree program locators, distance ...
www.linkopedia.com/Reference/Education/Distance_Learning/index.html Cached page

Fig 3.23: There is Linkopedia right at the top of MSN Search so that one is doing its job!

Radio Engineering
Educating hobbyists, enthusiasts and technophiles about digital radio technology
about digital radio technology. Website: http://www ...
www.worldsiteindex.com/wdird1641728334 Cached page 5/25/2005

Fig 3.24: Worldsiteindex has also worked.

The same command in Google gives a different result with Linkopedia nowhere to be seen!

Entertainment : Radio
Radio. ... Entertainment : Radio. Search for :. 1 - 5 of 5 entries. CDOX Radio
North Bay. Who is Doc? Doc is Lawrence Bishop who is on Dox Radio from ...
www.worldsiteindex.com/wdirc431913096 - 7k - Cached - Similar pages

searchsight.com/97A22S182P1-Oxfordshire-Books-Medi...
Similar pages

Fig 3.25: The Google result shows Worldsiteindex but not the other two.

3 Search Engine Submission

Radio Engineering
Educating hobbyists, enthusiasts and technophiles about digital radio technology.
http://www.radioeng.co.uk
More/Report/Modify

Fig 3.26: The entry in the World Site Index is part of a page listing several web sites.

Linkopedia is not there but both Worldsiteindex and Searchsight are missing so picking three directories has worked well as far as I am concerned. None of the directory listings have ever shown up in Yahoo but it doesn't seem to have impacted the ranking in that search engine.

Specialist Directory

You may have chosen a specialist directory while you were reading through chapter 1. If you didn't do so then please refer back to Figure 1.7.

Many of the free directories are now starting to charge for services. If you do decide to use one then check your entry as it may not be correct. Radio Dan (web site is www.radiodan.com) has hijacked the entry for the digital radio web site (www.radioeng.co.uk) in the Directory.

Radio Dan
RF Power Amplifiers & RF Exciters, ham radio etc (USA).
http://www.radioeng.co.uk/

Fig 3.27: The entry in the DirectoryRadio.com site is wrong. This is down to human error and was corrected.

Search Engine Submission 3

If I type the search query 'Radio Dan' into Google the digital radio web (Radioeng) site is number 4 in the search results. Obviously Google is giving entries in this Directory some weight as the phrase 'Radio Dan' never appears on the 'Radioeng' web site. It just shows how bizarre the actual indexing on the internet can be at times!

DMOZ

The Directory Mozilla (DMOZ) has or had the aim of producing a quality catalogue of all the web sites on the internet. It started as a Netscape idea and then became a volunteer driven project. The importance of DMOZ is declining and unless the delay in getting web sites reviewed improves dramatically it will cease to be important. If Google removes its support for the behemoth then it will fade away. I just don't bother with DMOZ any more. It will probably still help your ranking in Google but I would rather spend my time creating good content than interacting with DMOZ.

DMOZ is always looking for new editors and you can apply to be a category editor and it is a bit like writing a special CV for a job! You have to submit a detailed application and it is hard to create the impression that you are doing it for the greater good, which is what they are looking for. Unlike my listings I did get a prompt rejection notice to my own application!

Monitoring Progress

Later in the book you will learn how to monitor the ranking of your web site and pages in the search engines. It is worth doing this exercise every month to check on the effect of your changes and to make sure that your pages are not slipping down the rankings.

3 Search Engine Submission

Summary

At the end of this chapter you should now have submitted your web site to Google, Yahoo & MSN. ASK should find your web site if you have also submitted it to at least three general or global directories and one specialist directory. You have submitted or tried to submit your web site to DMOZ

Next Chapter

In the next chapter you will learn about some advanced techniques to check what has happened to your web pages. The internet is now huge and the search engines are devising more elaborate ways of assessing new web sites. You need patience and loads of it! Happily there are a few things that you can do to make things happen faster.

4. Advanced Techniques

If you have made all your changes and submitted your web site only to find that it is still 'invisible' in some of the search engines do rest assured that you haven't been singled out for special treatment! There may still be a problem or two with your web site.

Be prepared to get a little frustrated with the process, as after waiting patiently for one or two months you were expecting some positive results! You will be glad to hear that this is just another part of the overall challenge and there are still a few more avenues to consider and a few more things to try to get to the bottom of any problem. The secret is not to give up but to go on with the cycle of analysis, review and updating.

This is just the way of the web and you have to change your tactics and expectations to match how it works.

Checking the Indexes

The first thing to do is to check if your site has been indexed by any of the search engines. You have most likely typed in one or more of your search terms and scrolled through several pages of listing and just found nothing. There is a quicker way to check if your web pages are actually listed and it might give you a clue as to any problems.

To run a quick check you have to force a search engine such as Google to be site specific by typing the following command into the search window:

4 Advanced Techniques

site:www.radioeng.co.uk (or whatever your site is.)

Note that you only use the domain name and not the full URL description. In Google you can also drop the 'www' prefix and get the same results.

This should produce a result like the screenshot in Figure 4.1.

Fig 4.1: This confirms that the site has been indexed and that Google has picked up at least one Meta tag.

However you want to check a bit deeper as a one liner is a bit suspicious. The way to do this is to force Google to search on both the domain name and on a keyword from the site. This will tell you if the search engine robot is actually able to crawl through the site.

Typing in '**site:www.radioeng.co.uk digital+radio+mondiale**' (the two terms are separated by a space) will force Google, Yahoo, ASK or MSN to search for the web site plus the keywords to check if any actual web pages have been indexed.

Advanced Techniques 4

Remember to check each search engine separately and make a note of what you find. If this search fails to return any pages then you can be sure that even though Google and the other search engines have indexed the **web site** they have not crawled through it to find the **web pages.** This event has occurred for some reason and you may have to dig a little deeper to find a clue. Try some other searches using a different keyword– in this case a high level keyword of 'digital'. The search syntax is similar and as follows:

site:www.radioeng.co.uk digital – there is a space between the end of the domain name and the keyword.

While this search is also fruitless it does produce a clue as to why Google is having trouble. Google is fussy at the best of times so it is worth finding your site using similar direct access commands.

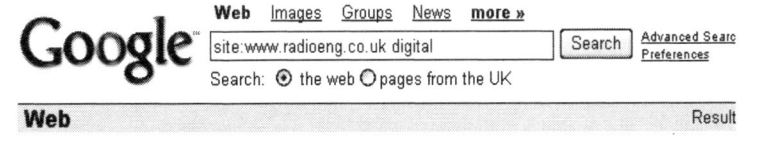

Fig 4.2: This is saying that Google has only found a single line of text from the site that was contained in a Meta tag.

The command should work in all the major search engines. ASK is the exception but just typing the domain in the search window by itself should produce a response.

4 Advanced Techniques

MSN produced very similar results (Fig 4.3) so there is a problem with the web site. Always check more than one search engine to determine where the problem might lie.

Web Results

1-1 of 1 containing **site:www.radioeng.co.uk** (0.16 seconds)

Digital Radio Technology
Educating hobbyists, enthusiasts and technophiles about digital radio technology. In order to view ... enabled browser.Page protected by Makesolutions ...
www.radioeng.co.uk Cached page

Fig 4.3: MSN's listing is just the same indicating a problem with the web site.

Google Spider Emulator

There is a handy tool that I think you need to be aware of that will tell you a bit about what the Google spider is picking up from your site.

The tool is called Poodle Predictor and is at http://www.gritechnologies.com/tools/spider.go

Here is a screen shot (Figure 4.4) from the Poodle tool. Poodle is pretty good at telling you what the Real Google engine will pick up. The various views such as Diagnostics and Source Code give you the chance to see what the HTML is saying in a lot more depth.

Advanced Techniques 4

Google is the fussiest of the search engines and I have often found the MSN and Yahoo spiders to be much more tolerant of errors.

The converse is then true: if your web pages can be navigated by the Google spider then you shouldn't have any problems with the other search engines.

Poodle _Predictor_ www.radioeng.co.uk

Enter your URL above to see what your site will look like in search-engine result
See how search-engine friendly your site is, can the spider crawl it easily? Will

Digital Radio Technology
In order to view this page you need a JavaScript enabled browser. Page
protected by Makesolutions - HTML/JavaScript Encoder. avaliable in...
www.radioeng.co.uk - 19k - Diagnostics View - Source-code View - Header

The spider found these links on the above page, the first 10 have been scanned,

Fig 4.4: The Poodle spider emulator's top level output shows that all the spiders are getting blocked.

Sure enough the site is not search engine friendly for Google or any other search engine. In this case Yahoo was able to extract quite a bit of information from the web site – you must check that all the 'big four' can crawl through your web site. The reason for this particular problem is that the pages are mostly written in a scripting language called PHP and was a bought-in script with 64-bit encoding, which was obviously too strong for Google and MSN. There is just too much server side scripting on the site and not enough HTML to provide the pathways through or around the encoded PHP.

4 Advanced Techniques

Digital Radio Technology
Quick Links IBOC DRM DTT DAB DR-SAT USA DR-SAT Europe ISDB Japan T-DMB If you are considering a DRM project then visit the DRM Consultancy.. www.radioeng.co.uk - k - Diagnostics View - Source-code View - Header-

Fig 4.5: A correct view from Poodle showing that a spider can now navigate the site.

Poodle has three views and the Diagnostics View shows you how a spider is going to work its way through your web site. You will be able to follow the links just like a spider so watch out for any error messages such as the one shown in Figure 4.6.

Warning: No h1, h2 or h3 Headings were found.
Digital Radio Mondiale Germany

Fig 4.6: Error message caused by the closing <h1> tags being missing.

Checklist 7

Here are a few more possibilities as to why some or all of your web pages are still invisible:

- Like the above example the web pages may be encoded in some way or are constructed using a lot of binary files. The advantage of using binary files is that the source code cannot be stolen as it is unreadable in Notepad and the web pages will execute a little quicker.

Advanced Techniques 4

- The file transfer process (FTP) has corrupted the process by transferring the files in the wrong mode.

- All the META data is the same so that the search engines have determined that most of your web pages are similar to one another and only a few have been added to the index.

- The robots haven't found the web site yet.

Accessing Your Server Logs

One of the things you really need to know is if the robot sent by the search engine is actually visiting your site. Don't assume that it is or that it has in the past. To find out for sure you will have to look at the server logs.

Hopefully your web hosting package has come with a comprehensive control panel, usually called cPanel or Plesk. Both offer similar facilities but I do find that cPanel has slightly more facilities and provides better logging information with a choice of analysis packages. Other hosting companies such as 1&1 have developed their own applications and they can be a bit more difficult to access.

Log into the control panel and then look for an icon called Web Stats or similar and if you are given the option then pick one of the Web/FTP statistics programs and run it. Look for an entry called Robots or Spiders and click on that and you should see something like Figure 4.7.

4 Advanced Techniques

Robots/Spiders visitors	
11 different robots	Hits
Inktomi Slurp	320+377
MSNBot	256+122
Googlebot	165+20
Unknown robot (identified by hit on 'robots.txt')	0+119
AskJeeves	69+19
LinkWalker	63+1
Unknown robot (identified by 'spider')	25+30
WISENutbot	44+2
Unknown robot (identified by 'crawl')	11+8
Unknown robot (identified by 'robot')	3+1
Voyager	1+1

Fig 4.7: List of spiders that visited a web site. Note that quite a few have not identified themselves.

Some logs are not as sophisticated as the display in Figure 4.7 and you might find an entry like this one shown in Figure 4.8.

Rank	Site	Accesses	%	Bytes	%
1	dsl-80-42-40-25.access.as9105.com	16	36.36	130,031	30.97
2	dsl-80-42-38-51.access.as9105.com	8	18.18	87,218	20.77
3	dsl-80-42-43-114.access.as9105.com	7	15.91	60,499	14.41
4	crawl31-public.alexa.com	5	11.36	60,920	14.51
5	tolra.force9.co.uk	4	9.09	53,960	12.85
6	4.79.40.166	1	2.27	0	0.00
7	host.aceofspace.com	1	2.27	0	0.00
8	64.210.196.197	1	2.27	13,597	3.24
9	msnbot.msn.com	1	2.27	13,597	3.24

Fig 4.8: Another form of log file output mixing the IP address with actual names.

Advanced Techniques 4

This information in Figure 4.8 is a bit harder to decipher as it is a mixture of IP addresses (the physical network address) and cryptic entries. However, you can see from the rank 9 entry that MSN (msnbot.msn.com) and from the rank 4 entry that the Alexa robot (crawl31-public.alexa.com) have been visiting. Alexa also uses the designation of Alexa (1A Archiver).

Google does tend to hide behind IP addresses so we don't know who 64.210.196.197 is. The web IP resolver stated that there was no reverse DNS entry for this one so we are none the wiser. If you have checked back through two month's worth of logs and can't clearly identify a robot or spider from the major search engines then it may be worth re-submitting your web site to the four major players.

293	1.62%	9	1.89%	crawl-66-249-66-173.googlebot.com
217	1.20%	10	2.11%	crawl-66-249-66-47.googlebot.com
194	1.07%	10	2.11%	crawl-66-249-65-148.googlebot.com
112	0.62%	4	0.84%	vm02-staging.alexa.com
119	0.66%	6	1.26%	crawl-66-249-66-19.googlebot.com
179	0.99%	9	1.89%	crawl-66-249-65-113.googlebot.com
30	0.17%	6	1.26%	egspd42254.ask.com
13	0.07%	0	0.00%	lj601711.inktomisearch.com

Fig 4.9: Yet another type of log, showing that Google, Alexa, Ask and Inktomi have stopped by. Note that 5 different Googlebots have visited this web site.

If you can work your way through 6 weeks worth of logs from your web site, sometimes looking up IP addresses at http://ww3.arin.net/whois/ to resolve some unknowns.

4 Advanced Techniques

Don't be surprised if you don't find every visitor and more importantly don't let it worry you as not every spider wants to make itself known to you. Most logs clearly showed visits from Netscape, Ask and Inktomi and so on and by looking back into the logs from a previous period you should find that Google had hit the site big time at some point.

Cast your mind back and you will probably find that the site had been very static during those months and it is likely that Google decided that nothing much had changed. It is unlikely that your site has been blacklisted but it is an outside possibility. Only you know if you have made multiple submissions in quick succession or tried other techniques that are viewed with suspicion.

If your web host does not provide the detailed analysis shown in the examples above you may be able to improve the situation by signing up to a free monitoring service where you place some additional code on each page that you want to monitor.

In the long run it may be better to move to a new hosting company that actually uses the cPanel interface. I have found this particular control panel to be one of the best available and worth the small extra cost levied by the hosting company.

The Robots File

One of the first things that any of these robots does is to look for a file called robots.txt in the highest level directory (usually the root directory on the www side of the site. You can create this file with Notepad or any other basic text editor – don't use WordPad or Word as it will add in too many other characters. The database of robots lists nearly 300 robots but luckily you will not be interested in that many.

Advanced Techniques 4

The major ones are:

Google	Googlebot
MSN	MSNbot
Yahoo	Slurp**
Alexa	Alexa (IA Archiver)
Inktomi	Slurp**
Looksmart	WISENutBot
Ask	AskJeeves

** Same robot.

The robot.txt file tells the robot how it can crawl through your site. This file can be used to exclude some or all of your web site from named robots or all robots. You need to get it right!

Web Statistics

Now that you have become familiar with accessing your web server logs you may want too check out the other information available. Some of this data is really useful and you should make a point of checking these logs once a month. Looking through the raw logs is time consuming and very confusing as server logs can make many events appear as error messages even when the action was carried out correctly. I wouldn't recommend that you download the raw logs if you are running on a Linux server as they will be in a format called 'tar-gzip' and the normal Windows unzipping utilities won't be able to open them. You therefore need a web-hosting company with an easy-to-use interface.

4 Advanced Techniques

Good web statistics will tell you the following:

- When the search engines visited the web site. However this may be restricted to the last visit.

- The number of referrals that have come from each named search engine.

- The number of links that are incoming to your site from other web sites.

- The better packages show full details of these incoming links.

- The search terms that are triggering hits on your web site as single keywords and keyword phrases.

- The popular landing pages or entry points to your web site.

- The files and pages that the visitors looked at.

- The locations of the real visitors.

- HTTP page errors, especially the 404 error that indicates that a page has not been found.

- The browsers that visitors are using. This may be important if you have only tested your web pages with a single browser. Certain communities have an affinity with Opera or Firefox rather than IE. Apple users have their own browser.

Advanced Techniques 4

Links from an external page (other web sites except search engines)	
Total: 20 different pages-url	
http://radioengnews.blogspot.com	5
http://www.users.waitrose.com/~bdxc/links.html	5
http://www.radio-digital.co.uk/links.php	3
http://203.84.199.31/language/translatedPage	2
http://www.drm.lap.hu	2
http://radioengnews.blogspot.com/2005_11_01_radioengnews_archive...	2
http://www.smartfind.org	2
http://203.84.199.31/language/translationHeader	1
http://64.233.179.104/translate_c	1
http://www.awt-inc.com/ez/index.php3	1
http://www.picsearch.com/info.cgi	1
http://radioengnews.blogspot.com/2006_03_01_radioengnews_archive...	1
http://www.birds-eye.net/definition/d/dmb-digital_multimedia_bro...	1

Fig 4.10: Part of a list of incoming links to the web site.

Like the other displays the actual presentation will vary from the example shown in Fig. 4.10.

Top 4 of 16 Total Referrers			
#			Referrer
1	81	17.92%	- (Direct Request)
2	16	3.54%	http://www.radio-digital.co.uk
3	8	1.77%	http://www.wave.webaim.org/wave/Output.jsp
4	4	0.88%	http://www.radioeng.co.uk/

Fig 4.11: This display provides less information but it is from a web site that is under development.

4 Advanced Techniques

The Customers

Countries (Top 25) - Full list				
Countries		Pages	Hits	Bandwidth
Great Britain	gb	413	2751	10.96 MB
United States	us	245	1309	7.50 MB
European Union	eu	61	792	3.43 MB
Spain	es	43	165	1.05 MB
Germany	de	39	410	2.59 MB
Russian Federation	ru	26	177	1.46 MB
France	fr	22	186	771.95 KB
Norway	no	20	96	438.69 KB
Unknown	ip	18	193	447.48 KB
Australia	au	16	92	992.26 KB
Japan	jp	12	151	736.10 KB
Canada	ca	12	86	364.46 KB
Ireland	ie	11	59	701.94 KB
Netherlands	nl	11	43	1.12 MB
Finland	fi	7	101	420.62 KB
Yugoslavia	yu	6	74	237.55 KB
Macedonia	mk	6	14	421.05 KB
Saudi Arabia	sa	5	33	353.60 KB
India	in	3	30	90.93 KB
Sweden	se	2	28	161.16 KB
Poland	pl	1	2	74.99 KB

Fig 4.12: This is a nice display showing where the visitors are based.

The important thing to look for in all these logs is that there is some activity. It takes time for the details of your web site and web pages to spread through the internet. Use this interval to get familiar with the statistics provided by your hosting company. This is useful information in that it confirms that real web users are finding your site and visiting it.

Advanced Techniques 4

Site Entry Points

Total: 59 different pages-url	Viewed	Average Size	Entry	Exit
/	447	14.48 KB	140	148
/digital-radio-mondiale.html	205	24.53 KB	100	81
/dmb.html	98	10.55 KB	61	52
/human-ear.html	36	11.62 KB	35	35
/audio.html	55	15.29 KB	33	31
/receivers.html	40	22.26 KB	28	22
/iboc.html	79	11.55 KB	28	26
/ofdm.html	24	26.23 KB	20	19
/worldspace.html	22	11.60 KB	19	16

Fig 4.13: Part of the site entry on landing points.

Some of these entries will have been generated by your own actions so watch out for them. The key piece of data that you are looking for is where in your site the visitors are arriving. If these entry points are deep in your site you may want to ensure that those pages are well linked to the other ones.

For example, you may have put a lot of effort into your home page whilst most of your returning visitors are going straight to a particular section of your product listing or to view old newsletters. This could mean that any targeted advertising is being missed and you might have to reconsider your whole promotional strategy.

Remember the point made in a previous chapter that landing pages should be self-contained with certain relevant information. You do not have much control over this as many links are referrals from an individual who has found your site to be interesting.

4 Advanced Techniques

Links from an Internet Search Engine	
10 different refering search engines	
Google	269
MSN	45
Yahoo	21
Google (Images)	19
Dogpile	2
Unknown search engines	1
Lycos	1
Seznam	1
Ask Jeeves	1
Netscape	1

Fig 4.14: This is saying that Google is providing most of the incoming traffic to the site. Netscape and Yahoo are familiar names and it might be interesting to check on Seznam.

Search Phrases

Keyphrases used on search engines
252 different keyphrases
t-dmb
human ear
the human ear
worldspace
t-dmb
digital multimedia broadcasting
eureka 147
digital radio mondiale
quadrature phase shift keying

Fig 4.15: Part of the key phrases list. The top of the page says that 252 different phrases have resulted in hits to this site

Advanced Techniques **4**

HTTP Error Codes

The HTTP error codes are worth knowing about as they may indicate that an error has occurred but not always! Usually they serve as indicators as to the health of a web site. Let me explain a few terms before looking at the list of codes.

HTTP stands for the Hyper Text Transfer Protocol and is the software specification that tells the web server and client PCs (via a web browser such as IE6) how to send data to and fro.

Resource: is anything that can be requested from the server. Typically this will be a file or document of some kind.

Request: will usually come from the client PC and gets the server to perform some operation such as reading a file or storing information in a database.

Proxy Server: is an intermediate relay server between the client PC and the actual resource. They can be deployed for security, speed and many other reasons.

Gateway: is a way of interfacing between two systems. There are payments gateways to credit card processors and also database gateways.

Protocol: is a set of rules that specifies how systems send information backwards and forwards. HTTP is a protocol.

Looking at the codes on the next few pages you can quickly see that many of them just confirm that the correct action has happened. Others are low level information and can just be ignored. There are just a few that will need you to take corrective action.

4 Advanced Techniques

Actual Code Numbers

The HTTP codes are divided into the following classes:

- 100/101 are just informational:
    - 100 means continue with the next action.
    - 101 tell the client or server to switch protocol.

- 2xx mean that a successful action has occurred:
    - 200: Successful request.
    - 201: Created a new resource such as a file.
    - 202: Accepted the request for processing.
    - 203: Low level information.
    - 204: No content to be returned as a result of the request.
    - 205: Reset content as would happen with an input form.
    - 206: Partial content issued when a multipart document is downloaded.

- 3xx indicates that the browser has been redirected to another URL to fulfil the request:
    - 300: user will be presented with a number of choices to reach the URL.
    - 301: The resource (file, image) has moved permanently to a anew URL.
    - 302: The resource was found under a different location.
    - 303: Go to a different URL.
    - 304: Access allowed but the document was not modified. This was a read only document.
    - 305: Use a proxy server.
    - 306: Not used yet.
    - 307: Temporary redirect.

Advanced Techniques 4

- 4xx are the actual client error codes:
    - 400: Bad request, not understood by the server.
    - 401: Request.
    - 402: Not used.
    - 403: Access forbidden as would happen with a password controlled directory.
    - 404: Resource not found.
    - 405: Method not allowed.
    - 406: Resource not able to give a response as the request is unacceptable.
    - 407: Proxy authentication required.
    - 408: Request timed out.
    - 409: Conflict: the request does not match the current state of the resource.
    - 410: Gone – resource no longer at server.
    - 411: Length of header required.
    - 412: Pre-condition failed.
    - 413: Requested resource is too large for server to process.
    - 414: URL too long.
    - 415: Unsupported media type.
    - 416: Range requested is too large.
    - 417: Proxy server error.

- 5xx are server errors:
    - 500: Internal error.
    - 501: Not used.
    - 502: Bad gateway.
    - 503: Service unavailable.
    - 504: Gateway timeout.
    - 505: HTTP version is not supported.

4 Advanced Techniques

Cracking the Code

As you can see from the list there are many error codes with more added each year. Thankfully the vast majority of these codes don't concern us and just a handful provides you with really valuable information about your site.

I analysed one of my sites over 5 months to see just how many of these codes came up in the web statistics and to see if they told me anything useful.

	May	April	March	February	January
206	99	73	85	75	35
301	89	131	99	86	56
302	99	190	93	233	213
401	8	17	4	0	0
403	3	8	0	0	0
404	91	157	182	35	30
405	0	0	2	0	0
500	0	20	24	0	0

Fig 4.16: Results of the error log analysis from a web site.

206 isn't really an error as it is confirming that a request for a multi-part document has been successfully executed. This is likely to be from the pages which were created with Word that stores any images in a separate folder or directory.

301 and **302** are informational that are recording that the client's browser has found pages that have moved. If you are constantly updating your site then you will always get some of these codes. I don't worry about 300 codes.

Advanced Techniques **4**

The Client Error Codes

The 400 series of codes are a lot more interesting so we will spend a little more time on them.

401 errors mean that somebody tried to get to a protected area of your site that requires some form of logon. This of course could have been a search engine robot if you haven't told them to avoid certain directories or it could be somebody poking around. Keep an eye on 401 errors.

If you start to see 30 or over per month in the logs then you do need to investigate what might be wrong.

One way to reduce the number of errors is to have a robots.txt file in the root directory that can be used to exclude any password protected directories from the robots.

A simple robots.txt looks like this:

User-agent: *
Disallow: /cgi-bin/
Disallow: /images/

This stops all robots (specified by the * in the user-agent field) from trying to spider the cgi-bin and images directories. You can create this simple file using Notepad and of course put in the names of the directories that you want to exclude.

403 is the server just refusing access to a particular resource. In my statistics these only appeared in April and May and could be linked to my own development work.

4 Advanced Techniques

405 errors say that there has been a violation of the HTTP protocol, which defines a set of particular operations for a web site. I remember generating this error as I tried to set up an automated mailing list function and the script was trying to send or POST data to the server.

404 errors are the ones that you need to study in bit more depth as they are telling you users are failing to find what they are looking for. Usually the web site statistics programme will give a bit more detail.

Required but not found URLs (HTTP code 404)	
URL (105)	Error Hits
/digital_radio_mondiale.html	10
/digital_terrestrial_television.html	7
/drm_english_broadcasts.html	7
/integrated_services_digital_br.html	6
/digital_radio_satellite_europe.html	6
/radio_engineering_publications.html	5
/sky_digital.html	4
/html/dmb.html	4

Fig 4.17: Pages not found probably because users of your web site have stored the now defunct page link as a favourite.

The screenshot in Figure 4.17 is from the www.radioeng.co.uk web site statistics. As the web site owner you will know if these are serious errors. All the errors listed above occurred because I removed all underlines as connectors and replaced them with hyphens. The error log should reduce month on month as problems are fixed and users update their browsers.

Advanced Techniques 4

ⓘ The page cannot be found

The page you are looking for might have been removed, had its name changed, or is temporarily unavailable.

Please try the following:

- If you typed the page address in the Address bar, make sure that it is spelled correctly.
- Open the www.radioeng.co.uk home page, and then look for links to the information you want.
- Click the ⇐ Back button to try another link.
- Click 🔍 Search to look for information on the Internet.

Fig 4.18: The familiar 404 error that gets displayed in a user's browser.

500 error codes are usually generated as you try to get scripts to work on your site. If you have a lot of them then you may need to contact your site administrator for some help. Sometimes this code is sent to the browser as an 'Internal Server Error'.

The script's documentation or the forum associated with the product may help resolve the issue. Usually it means that file permissions are incorrect and that the script or executable has not been allowed to run.

4 Advanced Techniques

Google AdWords

There are times when you have checked everything you can and you are still not successful in getting your web pages ranked by the search engines. This is happening more and more as the number of web sites increase and the search engines strive to find ways to improve the relevancy of the search engines results pages they offer to their customers. If you have determined that you are not being indexed correctly in the search engines then you need to do two things to bring the links and traffic to your site. The first thing that springs to mind is to plug the gap by paying for placements in the sponsored results sections of the search engines. The second thing that you do is to continue with the process of optimising your web pages. There are a huge number of PPC search engines but to be honest you are just wasting your money with the vast majority of them! You will recall from an earlier chapter that there are two big players in the Pay-Per-Click game and they are Google and Overture.

I recommend that you go for Google due to cost and their comprehensive on-line documentation facilities. Go to the site at http://adwords.google.com.First of all you need to create an account and then you can begin to set up your ad campaigns. Setting up a campaign is a three stage process although some of these stages have several sub stages. Don't worry about making errors as the Google system is very user friendly and loaded with guides and information and will warn you if the software detects that you are about to waste your money. Once you have set up a campaign you must check it once a day until you familiar with the overall process otherwise you are likely to run up a considerable amount of cost.

Advanced Techniques 4

Fig 4.19: Note that getting a paid for placement in Google also gets you into ASK plus one or two other minor or regional engines. The list changes from time to time.

Once you have a confirmed Google account you can being setting up your adverts. The first thing that you have to decide is which type of campaign you require. As Figure 4.20 shows there is now a choice between:

4 Advanced Techniques

- **Keyword targeted** where the advert is shown in response to keywords that you choose and where you are charged by Google only when a user clicks on the advert. This is the CPC or Cost-Per-Click mode.

- **Site targeted** where you can select sites from the Google network. The pricing model here is called CPM that stands for Cost-Per-Thousand and you get charged whenever the advert is shown.

All Campaigns

+ Create a new campaign: keyword-targeted | site-targeted [?]

| Pause | Resume | Delete | Edit Settings | Show all Campaigns |

Fig 4.20: Google now offers a choice of two advertising models.

Keyword Driven Campaign

The first step is the easiest of all. You choose your advertising language and the countries or regions you want to advertise in. Think about your requirement. Is this just aimed at the UK or do you want to have a global reach in the English language? You can always change this later on if you find that the initial settings haven't worked that well.

Advanced Techniques 4

Next you get to choose your countries. For this example I want to reach customers in the USA, UK and Canada.

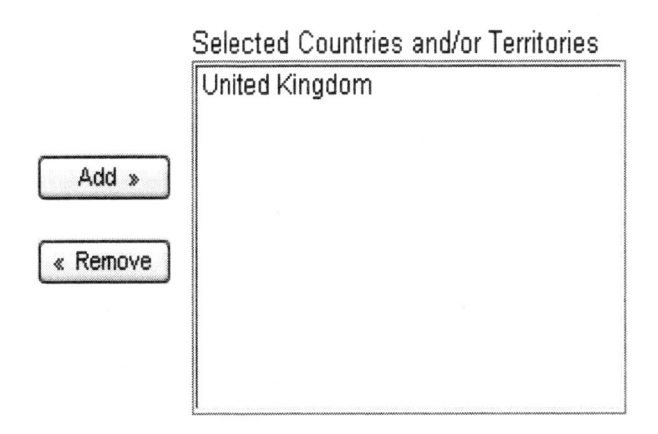

Selected Countries and/or Territories

United Kingdom

[Add »]

[« Remove]

Fig 4.21: Advert Campaign selected for the UK Only.

This is where you set up your advert and Google doesn't give you a lot to work with. You must have a really eye-catching Headline and then the next two lines have to achieve the following:

Line 1 has to offer the customer a benefit of some kind that also explains what your site is about.

Line 2 then tells the customer what else is on offer. You may want them to purchase something or entice them to sign up to an offer of a free newsletter. Google provides extensive help on this subject so do download and read it.

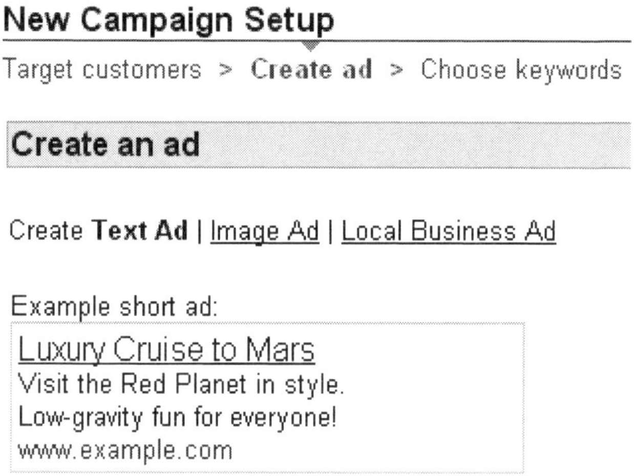

4 Advanced Techniques

New Campaign Setup

Target customers > **Create ad** > Choose keywords

Create an ad

Create **Text Ad** | Image Ad | Local Business Ad

Example short ad:

> Luxury Cruise to Mars
> Visit the Red Planet in style.
> Low-gravity fun for everyone!
> www.example.com

Fig 4.22: An example of a Google advert. They have to be succinct.

Once you have edited the text of your advert you have to choose the keywords that will trigger the display of your advert. Google helpfully offers you a list of possible keywords from its internal database. You can choose one or more of these or just enter your own. Choose them carefully as Google monitors the performance of each keyword and if enough people don't click on them then can get disabled.

Next you have to decide how much you are willing to pay for the keyword and Google levies a payment each time someone goes to your site via the ad. You also get to specify the maximum daily budget. Clicking on Calculate Estimates will allow you to check the effects of varying daily budgets and CPC costs will have on the ad position and the estimated daily traffic.

Advanced Techniques 4

If you are not getting a filled in bar graph in the Search Volume column then you should edit your keywords until you do.

The important thing to remember with Google is that the Clickthrough Rate (CTR) is the most important parameter for them as it a measure of how relevant your advert is. While you learn how to use Google Adwords be conservative with your CPC bids as you can quickly waste a lot of money.

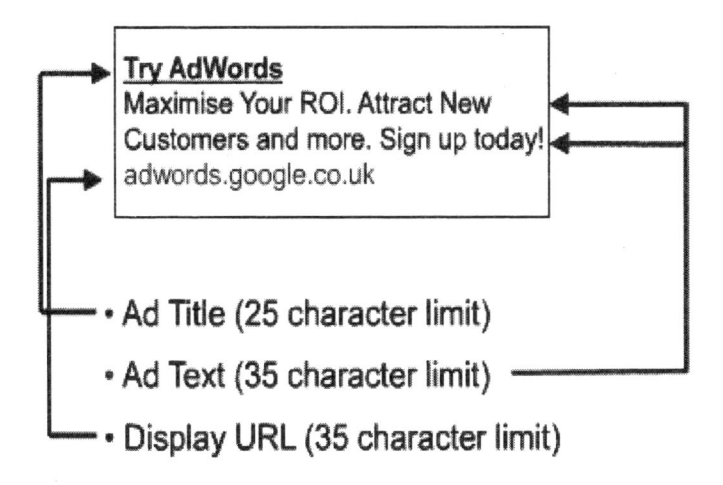

Try AdWords
Maximise Your ROI. Attract New Customers and more. Sign up today!
adwords.google.co.uk

- Ad Title (25 character limit)
- Ad Text (35 character limit)
- Display URL (35 character limit)

Fig 4.23: The Structure of a Google AdWord.

Keep this as a handy reference guide on how to create a good Google AdWord. Think how you would respond to your advert if you spotted it on a search results page.

4 Advanced Techniques

Estimates for the maximum CPC: £0.01 GBP and daily budget £1.00 GB

Keywords ▼	Predicted Status	Search Volume	Estimated Avg. CPC
Search Total			£0.00
digital radio broadcasting (Minimum £0.06)	Inactive for search		£0.00
digital radio mondiale (Minimum £0.03)	Inactive for search		£0.00

Estimates for these keywords are based on clickthrough rates for current advertisers. Google and may not trigger your ads until they are approved. Please note that your traf

Fig 4.24: The Google Traffic estimator will tell you what your minimum CPC should be.

Estimates for the maximum CPC: £0.03 GBP and daily budget £2.50

Keywords ▼	Predicted Status	Search Volume	Estimated Avg. CPC
Search Total			£0.03
digital radio	Active		£0.03
digital radio receivers	Active		£0.00

Estimates for these keywords are based on clickthrough rates for current advertise Google and may not trigger your ads until they are approved. Please note that your

Fig 4.25: Raising the CPC to the minimum specified by Google produces an improved level of confidence.

Advanced Techniques 4

Estimates for the GBP			
Keywords ▼	**Estimated Ad Positions**	**Estimated Clicks/Day**	**Estimated Cost/Day**
Search Total	**4 - 6**	**3 - 5**	**£1**
digital radio	4 - 6	3 - 5	£1
digital radio receivers	-	0	£0

Estimates for these kers. Some of the keywords above are subject to review by Google and may not f traffic estimates assume your keywords are approved.

Fig 4.26: The estimates now show that the advert will be on the first results page and likely to get up to 5 clicks per day. Note that these are estimates.

Success with Google AdWords will depend on the following four things:

- Choosing the best keywords to bid on. Use the tools outlined in Chapter 2 or just use the most relevant keywords from your web pages.

- Choosing just enough keywords. Start out with just two or three and adjust your campaign from there on.

- Bidding cleverly and working within a budget

- Creating good Ad Titles and Ad Text entries in your advert. If your advert isn't working then try swapping the text from the lines over. It can have a dramatic effect.

Don't be tempted to click on your adverts yourself as Google will detect that the clicks have come from you and may cancel your adverts and account.

151

4 Advanced Techniques

Campaign Summary > Campaign #1 > **Radio Engineering Publications**

Radio Engineering Publications Active | Pause Ad Group | Delete Ad Group
Current maximum CPC: **GBP £0.13** [edit]
09-Feb-2005 to 28-Feb-2005
Tools: ▶Filter Keywords | ▶Add Keywords | Edit Keywords | Keyword Tool

Digital Radio Mondiale Complex technology explained Free Newsletter. DRM Manual www.radioeng.co.uk	+ Create New Text Ad	Image Ad 6 Clicks	0.9% CTR	£0.05 CPC Served - 58.1% [more info] Edit - Delete	○ today ◉ 9 ▾ Feb ☐ Include deleted

Delete | Edit CPCs/URLs

☐ **Keyword**	**Status**	**Clicks ▾**	**Impr.**	**CTR**
Search Total		6	853	0.7%
Content Total		3	186	1.6%
☐ Digital Radio Mondiale	Normal	4	252	1.5%
☐ IBOC	Disabled	2	507	0.3%
☐ Digital AM	Normal	0	52	0.0%
☐ Digital Shortwave	Normal	0	42	0.0%

Lower CTRs for content ads will not adversely affect your campaign. [more info]
Reporting is not real-time. Clicks and impressions received in the last 3 hours may not be included here.

Fig 4.27: The campaign summary section provides extensive statistics

Figure 4.27 is an example of the level of detail provided by Google when running an advertising campaign. Some of the keywords have been disabled by Google as the level of usage hasn't reached Google's threshold and they have been automatically disabled.

Advanced Techniques 4

Site Targeted Campaign

The second type of advertising is to closely target the sites that run Google adverts.

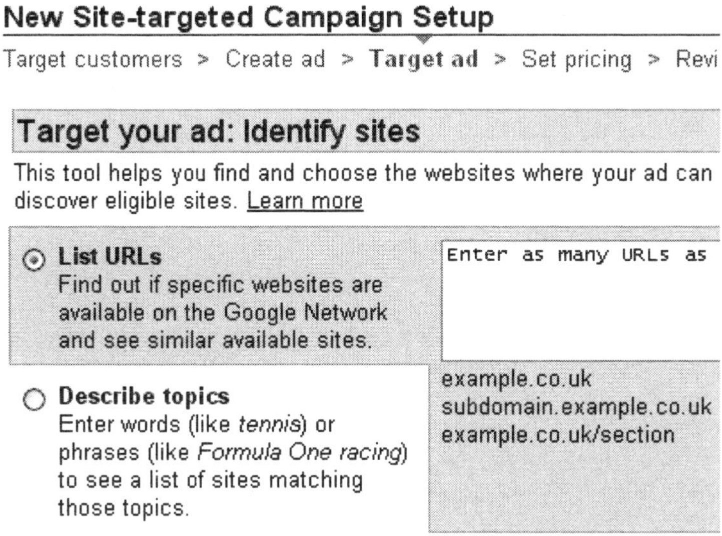

New Site-targeted Campaign Setup

Target customers > Create ad > **Target ad** > Set pricing > Revi

Target your ad: Identify sites

This tool helps you find and choose the websites where your ad can discover eligible sites. Learn more

- ⊙ **List URLs**
  Find out if specific websites are available on the Google Network and see similar available sites.

  Enter as many URLs as

- ○ **Describe topics**
  Enter words (like *tennis*) or phrases (like *Formula One racing*) to see a list of sites matching those topics.

  example.co.uk
  subdomain.example.co.uk
  example.co.uk/section

Fig 4.28: The best way forward now is to work by topics as this will give you a list of web sites together with how popular they are.

Note how the use of topics rather than individual words is entering more and more of Google's work. Before you just jump in and pick the web sites with the highest figures I would recommend that you visit them to check that they match your values and the message that you want your web pages to convey.

4 Advanced Techniques

24	arionradio.com	0k-10k	Add »
25	lyrics.com	10k-100k	Add »
26	dishant.com	10k-100k	Add »
27	smashitsusa.com	10k-100k	Add »
28	flowers.com	10k-100k	Add »
29	flatcast.com	0k-10k	Add »
30	non-standard.net	10k-100k	Add »
31	music.com	10k-100k	Add »
32	di.fm	10k-100k	Add »

Fig 4.29: List of web sites by topic showing the number of page impressions per day.

Finally, I want to emphasise a few points about the use of Google Adwords. By using this system you are competing with other advertisers to get your advert in a prominent position on the Google search engine results pages. The content and quality of your web site has now assumed a secondary importance as far as the Google search engine is concerned but users who click through to your web site or web page are still going to expect to find good content and a well laid out web site. The other search engines such as Yahoo and MSN are not usually part of the Google advertising system but ASK has participated from time to time. I have only used Google AdWords as a stop-gap measure to give me time to improve my web pages so that they will appear in the organic listings. If your strategy and budget is different then there is no reason not to continue with an ongoing Google campaign.

Advanced Techniques 4

Daily budget: GBP £2.50   [Edit]

> **Ad Group name:** test2   [Edit]
>
> **Ads:**
>
> > Digital Radio Explained
> > Learn About Digital Radio
> > Free newsletter; PDF Courses
> > www.radioeng.co.uk
> >
> > Edit - Delete
>
> **Sites:**   [Edit]
>
> radioblogclub.com   mediauk.com
>
> **Maximum CPM:** GBP £0.15   [Edit]

Fig 4.30: This is the point where you push your advert into the Google Network.

Google Network

The Google Network is basically made of web sites that have signed up to the Google AdSense programme. Here a member makes available space on his or her web pages to allow Google to place adverts generated in the AdWords programme. In this case Google pays the web site owner to host the adverts using calculations similar to those applied to the advertisers. This is something that you may want to consider as a way of generating income or of adding value to your web pages.

4 Advanced Techniques

ut **141,000** for **digital radio** mondiale. (0.34 seconds)

Sponsored Links

Shortwave Info Center
PC shortwave radios, portables
WorldStation software, free info
www.dxtra.com

Digital Radio Mondiale
Complex technology explained
Free Newsletter. DRM Manual
www.radioeng.co.uk

Fig 4.31: The advert appeared on the first page of the Google search engine's results

Does it Work?

Yes it does! The Google adverts that I have created generally appear in a few minutes. Figure 4.31 is an actual screenshot and I can see links to my site coming in from sites like the Chicago Tribune that also taps into the extensive Google ad network. Using Google Adwords saved my bacon whilst I wrestled with indexing and other problems! I have no hesitation in recommending it as a worthwhile tool.

Advanced Techniques 4

Checklist 8

There are few quick checks that you can carry out to determine how well the search engines have crawled your web site.

- Use the 'site' command in each of the four major search engines just to see if they have picked up any web pages. Note any strange error messages.

- Check your server logs to see what search engine robots have visited your web site.

- Check your server logs for any error messages that need immediate attention.

- Run your web site through Poodle to make sure that the spiders can actually crawl through the site.

- Gather whatever information you can so that you can research the problem.

- Wait another month as you may have been missed in this month's crawl.

- Consider using Google AdWords as a way of getting visibility while you sort out the problems.

- Using Google AdSense may generate revenue to offset your advertising costs.

4 Advanced Techniques

Summary

There are a few points to note as a result of all this trawling through logs.

- Do take note of the 404 errors as it is indicative of users have problems with your site. Fixing some will be easy and others will take a bit of effort on your part. It is worth it as it makes the customer experience better.

- When you update your site do test it as thoroughly as you can. It is better that you find the errors and not your customers.

- Be aware that moving from one format to another (in my case from PHP to HTML) can cause problems for users who have book marked your site.

Next Chapter

In the next chapter I will show you how to optimize your web pages for each of the major search engines. You will probably want to apply the general optimization advice in the first instance and then work on each of the search engines in turn.

5. Search Engine Optimization

You will come across various terms for the process of using search engines to draw traffic to your web site but Search Engine Optimization or SEO for short is the one in most common usage. The increase in traffic is achieved by influencing the spider or robot based search engines through modifications to your web pages.

Applying Optimization

The web page optimization process can be divided into <u>general advice</u> applicable to most search engines and <u>specific advice</u> for the four major families of search engines. Following the general advice will make a difference but if you can apply the specific advice then you really will see a difference in your rankings. This next statement may be obvious but if you want to rank highly in a particular search engine then use the specific advice for that engine. Alternatively, if you want to rank as high as possible in all the search engines then start with the general optimization advice and if that doesn't achieve your objectives then I can only recommend that you optimise a few pages for each search engine and make sure that you have a very efficient navigation structure to get your visitors to all the pages. If you have a web site structured along the lines suggested in chapter 2 then you may be able to use the overlapping theme to achieve high rankings across the board without having to create any new pages. Don't be tempted to create the same page four times to try to optimize each version for one of the major search engines. This may be interpreted as a form of 'cloaking' where different pages are presented to users and search engines.

5 Search Engine Optimization

There are a number of stages to the process of search engine optimization (SEO):

- Search Engine Visibility where the webmaster sweeps away the major blocks to the site being visited and indexed by the robot. We have covered most of this in the preceding chapters. Even though the robots will visit and store the web pages there is no guarantee that they will be added to the index.

- Search Engine Optimization (Internal to the web page) where the quality of individual pages is improved by editing the content and meeting the parameters of the search engines. The aim of this stage is to get the pages included in the index. Once in the index the robot will visit regularly and the work carried out on improving the site will bear dividends.

- Search Engine Optimization (External to the web page) where the standing of our web page is increased by getting good quality links into the web page or web site.

- Search Engine Marketing where the above stages are combined with internet analytics and paid advertising to create an integrated approach to making the web pages highly visible to the target audience.

The fourth stage is left to last as if you can achieve all your objectives through stages one to three then you are likely to have done it all for free without having to pay for specialist advice or expensive advertising.

Search Engine Optimization **5**

General Optimization Advice

This section is about making a set of changes that will make a positive difference in all the search engines. There are three aspects to the optimization process and they are called:

- On the Page Factors such as the content of the key HTML tags and the body text and so on. These factors are under your direct control.

- Off the Page Factors that you have less control over as they are created by other people and systems. However you can influence them to some degree by approaching webmasters in a considerate way. Of course, if your web pages are packed full of good, original content then other webmasters will link to you and boost your rankings.

- Page URL Factors such as having the keyword in some part of the page URL. Ideally, if your domain name has the keywords it in as well this is viewed as a positive factor.

    Here are some examples of what I mean:

Page URL	**Rating**
www.cheap-tools.com/cheap-tools.html	✓✓✓
www.cheaptools.com/cheap-tools.html	✓✓
www.cheaptools.com/cheapt_tools.html	✓
www.cheaptools.com/cheaptools.html	✗

161

5 Search Engine Optimization

On The Page Factors

<HEAD> Region

The first area we need to consider is <HEAD></HEAD> region of the web page where the search engine robots examine the content of three tags. First of all the robots are going to look at the robots.txt file to see if they are restricted in what they can index on the web site. I cover this topic in the next chapter and as it has little to do with the theory of SEO, I will skip over it for now.

<TITLE> Tag

The first and very important tag is the 'Title' tag contained between the HTML markers of <TITLE> and </TITLE>. This is a very important piece of information for all the robots as it is the first clue as to the theme of your web page. The information contained within the tag is displayed at the very top of a web browser in what is called the caption bar. You must have a well thought out sentence as this tag and your aim should be to make it the slogan for that web page, something that people will remember. Therefore strip out any stop words. A stop word is a common word that has no contextual meaning. 'It', 'is', 'and', 'or' and so on count as a word and dilute some of the metrics calculated by the search engine robots.

Search engines examine the keywords in this tag and give them a lot of weight. You should use your primary keyword at the start of the text and a secondary or synonym at the end. In total you should try to limit the overall word count to around 10 words although the range can be anywhere between 5 and 15 words. Try to create a slogan for each of your web pages.

Make sure that the <Title> is the first tag in the <head> region and use only a single <title> tag. As indicated previously you should create a different <title> tag for each page as this is what is displayed in the search engine results.

META Description Tag

The information in this tag is what most search engines will display under the <title> information in a search engine hit or result. If there is nothing in this tag the search engine will create one from other data on that web page. The description should be brief but inform the web user about the content or purpose of this web page. Include keywords and keyword phrases if you can and limit the overall length of the tag to around 30 words.

There should be a separate description tag for each web page.

META Keyword Tag

Many search engines seem to have abandoned using the information contained in this area. Nevertheless, I usually put a primary keyword and a secondary keyword here just for completeness.

Keyword Metrics

I now want to show you how a search engine will calculate three parameters called **keyword frequency, keyword density or weight, keyword prominence and keyword proximity.**

5 Search Engine Optimization

Keyword frequency

This is the easiest one to understand and work out manually even when there is a large amount of text. The parameter is calculated for an area of text that may be a single sentence or a whole page.

The keyword frequency is the number of times a keyword is used in the area of text being analysed.

Working with the example of '**Get the Cheapest Lawnmowers at Fred's Garden Emporium**' in the <title> tag and a keyword phrase of '**Cheapest Lawnmowers**' the keyword frequency of the word 'Cheapest Lawnmowers' is 1 as it occurs just once between the title tags.

It doesn't matter how many words are in the phrase – if the keyword phrase is 'Fred's Gardening Emporium' then the frequency is still one.

Keyword Weight

Calculating keyword weight or density is a bit more complicated but it can still be done manually. Still working with the example of '**Get the Cheapest Lawnmowers at Fred's Garden Emporium**' and a keyword phrase of '**Cheapest Lawnmowers**' the keyword weight is calculated as follows:

Keyword frequency multiplied by **the number of words in the keyword** divided by **the total number of words in the area**

For the phrase above KWW= $\frac{1 \times 2}{8}$ (x100) = 25%

Search Engine Optimization 5

Removing the stop words of 'get' 'the' and 'at' changes the title to: **Cheapest Lawnmowers Fred's Garden Emporium'**.

For the phrase above KWW= $\frac{1 \times 2}{5}$ (x100) = 40%

If '**Fred's Garden Emporium**' is also a keyword phrase then its KWW is:

For the phrase above KWW= $\frac{1 \times 3}{5}$ (x100) = 60%

After this the choices are getting limited and there may be little more that you can do.

```
<!DOCTYPE HTML PUBLIC "-//W3C//DTD HTML 4.0 T
<HTML>
<HEAD>
<TITLE>Digital Radio Technology equals Radio
<META HTTP-EQUIV="Content-Type" CONTENT="text
<META NAME="Author" CONTENT="Kevin Ryan">
<META NAME="Abstract" CONTENT="Educating hobk
<META NAME="Copyright" CONTENT="KPR i-service
<META NAME="contact_addr" CONTENT="PO Box 243
<META NAME="Description" CONTENT="Digital rac
<META NAME="Date" CONTENT="20 September 2005"
<META NAME="Keywords" CONTENT="digital radio
<META NAME="Generator" CONTENT="NetObjects Fu
<META NAME="Robots" CONTENT="ALL">
<LINK REL=STYLESHEET TYPE="text/css" HREF="./
<LINK REL=STYLESHEET TYPE="text/css" HREF="./
<STYLE>
</STYLE>
</HEAD>
```

Fig 5.1: The <HEAD> region of a web page.

5 Search Engine Optimization

The advice is that you really cannot handle more than two keyword phrases at a time otherwise the KWW value gets distributed too thinly. You may decide just to have a single keyword phrase in the title and this will always yield 100%. My recommendation is that you work with two keywords: a primary one for the page theme and a secondary one that overlaps with another web page and is a synonym of that page's primary keyword.

Exercise 9

Try to determine the effect of having the title below in the <HEAD> region.

Title: Cheapest Lawnmowers Cheapest Lawnmowers

The question is whether you can improve the KWW factor beyond 100%?

Answer: No, as you can't get more than 100%.

Keyword Prominence

This is the most difficult of all the keyword metrics to understand and calculate. Prominence is the proximity of the keyword or keyword phrase to the start of the area being analysed. This is harder to calculate manually but you can work out a good approximation by visually inspecting the area of text provided that it does not contain too many words. We are still working with our now familiar title of **Get the Cheapest Lawnmowers at Fred's Garden Emporium**' and a keyword phrase of '**Cheapest Lawnmowers'** as this contains a nice round figure of eight words and two words respectively. This will make the calculations easier.

Search Engine Optimization 5

Get	The	Cheapest	Lawnmowers	At	Fred's	Garden	Emporium
W1	W2	KW3	KW4	W5	W6	W7	W8
100%		**75%**		50%		25%	
							←

Fig 5.2: Work out the prominence figures by working from the end of the sentence as the arrow shows you.

Keyword Example 1

Working with Figure 5.2 you can see that the keyword phrases have been identified as KW3 and KW4. The title phrase has been split into pairs of words. To understand the concept of proximity to the start of the phrase it is best to work from the other end in the direction of the arrow. The last two words are the furthest away from the start of the title phrase so they get the lowest score.

A formula would look something like this as the wanted keyword phrase (KW3 & KW4) is in the position three (3) of a possible four (4).

$$\text{For the phrase above KWP} = \frac{3}{4}(\times 100) = 75\%$$

If words W1 & W2 are removed the wanted keyword phrase moves forward to position 3 of a possible 3 and the keyword prominence goes up to 100%.

Try out some examples of your own from the data on your web site to build your understanding of this parameter. We need to consider another example to see how the keyword prominence varies with different numbers of words.

5 Search Engine Optimization

Keyword Example 2

Consider a META keyword entry that has just two keywords that are 'digital audio broadcasting' and its acronym 'DAB'. This time we cannot split the words into nice equal pairs or triplets.

Each keyword is analysed in a slightly different way. The digital audio broadcasting keyword's prominence is 100% as it is right at the start of the phrase. This should make perfect sense.

One might have thought that DAB would have a prominence of 50% as it, is after all, the other keyword of the only two used. However for the DAB keyword the other words are just words and DAB is in the last position of a possible 4 so the prominence is 25%.

Digital	Audio	Broadcasting	DAB
W1	W2	W3	KW4
			25%

Fig 5.3: Prominence is not always what it seems.

<BODY> TAG

The same metrics will be applied to the body text that will contain many hundred words. With the help of a highlighter pen you can calculate keyword frequency and keyword weight to a reasonable degree of accuracy. By making sure that your keywords are in the first twenty-five words of text you are going to achieve a keyword prominence of between 95% and 100% in any case so you don't need to spend time trying to work it out. If you really want to know then you should get your hands on one of the packages from chapter 6.

Search Engine Optimization 5

There are recommendations for keyword density and keyword weight in the body text but you should write naturally and not force up the frequency by repetition or other contrived means. This area is for the human visitor and should be constructed without any thought of a robot! If you want a target to aim for then keyword weight should be at least 2%. For small areas of text with niche information it can be as high as 10%.

If you have used the **HEADER tags** <H1> to <H6> then make sure that the text under the headers really belongs there. Don't stuff the headers with your keywords and then put unrelated content underneath.

Look up the **synonyms** for your keywords as some search engines take these into account for the keyword parameters. If your content is about computers then you may want to use PC, desktop, laptop, processor and server and so on.

Resist the use of **abbreviations** or **acronyms** unless you are absolutely sure that the abbreviation or acronym is unique and well known in your target areas. I write extensively about digital radio where Digital Radio Mondiale (DRM) is one of the standards. Unfortunately DRM is also the abbreviation for Digital Rights Management.

If you have used images then the **ALT tag**, if you can get at it should contain a description of the image as well as one of your page keywords.

Link text is the text seen in the visible part of a link and is also called anchor text. For outbound links make sure that you include some of your keywords, especially if you are linking to another page in your web site.

5 Search Engine Optimization

Checklist 9

- I need to remove stop words from the title and keyword Meta tags.

- I have more than two keywords on some pages and will work to reduce this to just one or two.

- I have keywords in header text but they bear no relationship to the text underneath them.

- I have blank or nonsensical ALT image text.

- I have no keywords in bold or in italic text.

- I do not use any synonyms or the alterations of the keywords. By alterations I mean expansion of the stem word.

- I am using a lot of abbreviations or acronyms that could have other expansions. For example DRM expands to Digital Radio Mondiale & Digital Rights Management.

- I have not written the body text in my natural style but have tried to think like a search engine.

- I have no link text other than arrows or phrases like 'more' or 'click here'.

- The keyword weight in the body text is below 2%. I will edit the content to improve on this figure.

Off The Page Factors

Once you have done all you can with each individual page the next step is to consider any 'off the page factors' that you can influence.

It is not always possible to make changes as webmasters do not answer every request made of them or will just decide that they don't want to link to your web site without giving a reason. To improve your chances of getting these vital incoming links you need to check that your theme is consistent across your whole web site and that there is some overlap in the themes of the individual web pages. This will encourage webmasters to rate your web pages highly and link to one or more of your web pages. The other major factor is the quality of the link or anchor text. Sometimes you can contact the writer of the link text and get them to put in one of your keywords. On many occasions the link to one of your web pages has been put in a forum entry and the author is not inclined to find and edit their contribution.

Specific Optimization Advice

Each of the major search engine families have particular parts of the web page that they analyse in slightly different ways. The next few sections give advice on adjusting a web page to meet the requirements of a particular search.

You will find that some of the suggestions cannot be met in all search engines. Where there isn't a specific recommendation on a page area such as title then just apply the general optimization advice that you have already read.

5 Search Engine Optimization

MSN Optimization

On The Page Factors

Please remember that these are recommendations. The data has been obtained mainly by the analysis of the top ranking sites in MSN and should be taken as a guide to why MSN ranked this site in the top 20 sites. If your web site already has a high ranking in MSN then I advise that you proceed with caution and carefully consider any change.

MSN still places considerable weight on the keywords that you place in the META keyword tag. This is probably the one factor where MSN is most at odds with the other search engines. MSN will use as many as 50 keywords in this tag. This does mean that MSN is not applying keyword metrics such as weight and prominence to this tag but is using the keywords as almost a summary of the page's content.

If you are optimising for the other major search engines then I would suggest that you put no more than 8 to 10 keywords in this tag. MSN also has an optimum page size of about 500 to 800 words. This is a statistical analysis so there will be pages with more and fewer words than these. I have a page on digital radio that ranks as number 1 in MSN and it has 1125 words, which is well outside this mean value range.

Again, if your page is in the top 10 then prune back 5% or so whilst trying not to remove too many of your keywords at the same time. If pages from your web site are actually at number 1 then why change anything? MSN's own advice is that it values content above all else. The first and last paragraphs of your web page are very important and you should try to fill them with the keywords that best describe the page's content.

Search Engine Optimization 5

The first 25 words that will usually be contained in the opening two sentences carry particular weight. You should also try to close out the page with one or two sentences that are rich in keywords.

Before you do this, you should check the path that a search engine robot will take through your web site by using the tools suggested in chapter 6.

The body text is still important to the MSN robot but you shouldn't make this unreadable or just downright uninformative to meet a key metric. The general consensus is that a keyword weight of around 3% should be your target.

MSN may have an overall page size after which it will stop ingesting your content for analysis. I don't think that many web pages will exceed the limit of about 150-200 Kbytes, as even with some graphics (apparently MSN doesn't count these) you are rarely going to exceed this value.

Name	Size	Type	Modified
dab1.html	9KB	HTML D...	22/02/2006 18:10
digital-radio-mondiale-d...	44KB	HTML D...	22/02/2006 18:10
digital-radio-mondiale.html	30KB	HTML D...	07/04/2006 17:03
digital-radio-satellite-eur...	9KB	HTML D...	22/02/2006 18:10
digital-radio-satellite-usa...	9KB	HTML D...	22/02/2006 18:10
digital-terrestrial-televisi...	15KB	HTML D...	22/02/2006 18:10
digital-video-broadcasti...	11KB	HTML D...	22/02/2006 18:10
digital_radio.html	17KB	HTML D...	10/01/2006 18:27

Fig 5.4: You can find out the size of your web pages in a number of ways. This is from an FTP programme.

5 Search Engine Optimization

📄	photoview.php	4.00 KB
📄	poll.php	4.00 KB
📄	postguest.php	40.0 KB
📄	printfag.php	4.00 KB
📄	readme.txt	64.0 KB
📄	readme_agenda.txt	4.00 KB
📄	reco.php	8.00 KB
📄	robots.txt	4.00 KB
📄	search.php	20.0 KB
📄	stats.php	4.00 KB

Fig 5.5: You can also check file size via your hosting control panel's File Manager.

The text you put in your internal links should also be rich in your keywords but don't forget that presentation to your reader is also important. Aim to have 6 to 15 words in these links to other parts of your site. The best way to do this is to communicate with the webmasters on the linking sites to suggest improvements to the link text.

Off The Page Factors

MSN focuses on link quality rather than link quantity. The incoming link should be from a related site that has a theme like your one or has some basic connection to your site. Just having loads of links from any free directory won't add much value and MSN will ignore them.

Search Engine Optimization 5

I have web pages that vary in rank between 1 and 5 in MSN on digital radio that have just half a dozen links incoming. The links that matter most are from a niche Radio Directory and from the Digital Radio Mondiale consortium of which I am a paid member and supporter. The site is also listed in three general directories and I know that a handful of radio clubs also have links to this site.

Summary For MSN

Factor	Recommendation
META Keywords	About 8-10 but can be as many as 50. Put your top one or two keywords at the beginning.
META Title	Keyword prominence of 50% and as high a weight as possible.
Body text	500-800 words.
Body: keyword weight	3%
Text Links	6-15 words with keywords.
Incoming Links	Ideally about 6 as a minimum.
Link Quality	Sites with a related theme are better.
Page size limit	< 200 Kbytes.

ASK Optimization

ASK's own advice is that it values content above all else. The first and last paragraphs of your web page are very important and you should try to fill them with the keywords that best describe the page's content. The first 25 words that will be contained in the opening two sentences carry particular weight. You should also try to close out the page with one or two sentences that are rich in keywords.

5 Search Engine Optimization

The body text is still important to the ASK robot but you shouldn't make this unreadable or just downright uninformative to meet a key metric. The general consensus is that a keyword weight of around 3% should be your target.

ASK may have an overall page size after which it will stop ingesting your content for analysis. I don't think that many web pages will exceed the limit of about 150-200 Kbytes, as even with some graphics you are rarely going to exceed this value.

Summary For ASK

Factor	Recommendation
META Keywords	Just use one or two keywords so that they are as prominent as possible.
META Title	Prominence of keywords to be 50% as a minimum.
Body text	250-500 words.
Body: keyword weight	3% - 10%
Text Links	6-15 words.
Incoming Links	6 minimum.
Link Quality	Sites with a related theme get better ranking.
Page size limit	< 200 Kbytes.

The site's theme is an important factor for ASK and you should put some extra effort into the 'human' factors such as high quality content.

Search Engine Optimization 5

Yahoo Optimization

Yahoo is still keen on META tag information so make sure that all these elements comply with the advice in the book. Yahoo likes to see a very descriptive title that is very informative and much longer than most other search engines. Apart from that one issue the general optimization advice seems to work well with Yahoo.

Summary For Yahoo

Factor	Recommendation
META Keywords	Prominence of at least 50% with a high weight.
META Title	Descriptive with up to 20 or 30 words.
Body text	250-500 words.
Body: keyword weight	2%
Text Links	6-15 words.
Incoming Links	6 minimum.
Link Quality	High quality links.
Page Size Limit	<200 Kbytes

Google Optimization

In addition to the factors listed in summary below it is likely that Google uses changes in these key metrics in their secret algorithms. The list of possible factors is literally huge and here are the major ones that have been recently discovered by researchers.

5 Search Engine Optimization

- Frequency of changes to a web page. Luckily it is now possible to let Google have information about how often you change your web pages via the Google sitemaps facility.

- The degree of the changes. A major re-working of a web page seems to be viewed with suspicion! With Google it may be better to create a completely new page and then phase out the old one when the new web page has been accepted into the index.

- A change in keyword density.

- The way links to your web pages change and develop. It seems to be better if link growth is natural and at a steady pace as that would reflect a process of natural discovery and recommendation. Rapid growth could be down to an active campaign of link promotion and therefore somewhat artificial.

- How long you have registered your domain name.

- The anchor text found in the links to your web pages. Google looks for varied anchor text as this reflects real recommendation rather than link swapping or some other forced process.

- Address of the web site owner. It is rumoured that Google keeps a list of known spammers or advocates of 'black hat' SEO techniques.

- The number of pages on the web site. If you have followed the advice given in chapter 2 then you will not have any problems.

Overall Google is trying to find web pages that are being discovered and rated by human beings who then promote the site via a link to it.

Summary For Google

Factor	Recommendation
META Keywords	Keyword prominence >50%
META Title	Keyword prominence >60%
Body text	250-500 words
Body: keyword weight	4% - 7%
Text Links	6-15 words
Incoming Links	6 minimum

Summary

Each of the major search engines have their own algorithms that they apply to your web pages. The details of these algorithms are kept secret and much of the current advice is generated by analysing the characteristics of the web sites that are being ranked in the top 10 or top 20 search engine results.

Next Chapter

The next chapter is a review of the tools that you can download and use to make the analysis of your web pages that much easier. Many of the free tools will provide all the functionality you need to optimize your web pages so download and use them.

6. Advanced Tools

Calculating or just estimating some of the optimization metrics can quickly get to be a tiresome task. When your body text gets to 500 words or more you need to save time by using a software tool. Some of the metrics such as **keyword frequency** are easy to work out as you just need to count words and get your results from some simple arithmetic. Once you get to something like **keyword prominence** then I recommend that you acquire at least one software package to help you with the calculations. The good news is that many of the free versions provide very comprehensive reports that are more than adequate for personal use.

The key areas that most integrated packages offer are:

- Keyword Analysis
- Keyword Suggestion
- Search Engine Ranking
- Top 10 Analysis
- General Page Optimization
- Specific Page Optimization
- Link Popularity
- Spider Simulation

I have found that the keyword checking facilities vary considerably between packages. You will find some freeware tools that help with some of these tasks and a number of web sites offer one-off analysis of individual pages. In some cases this may be all you need but if you are going to have a programme of continuous improvement then you will probably need to buy a software package.

Advanced Tools 6

Browsers

If you are developing web sites then it is worth having the following browsers on your PC. Happily, they all work in harmony today so you don't have to worry about them overwriting each other. Just make sure that you set your favourite browser as the default one.

Internet Explorer

You should have IE6 on your PC already but if not then you can download a copy from Microsoft. The latest version is available at: www.microsoft.com/windows/ie/ie6/downloads/default.mspx.

IE7 is soon to be released and it looks like this version will look and feel completely different to IE6.

Firefox

This is an up and coming challenger to the dominance of IE6. You can download a copy from: http://www.mozilla.com/firefox/.

Opera

This is another favourite and you can get a copy from this URL: http://www.opera.com/.

Lynx

Lynx is a useful tool but it is not much use as a browser. The screenshot in Figure 6.1 shows how the standard Google interface would look in Lynx. I use it as a quick way of checking that a spider can navigate a web site. I would not use it for any serious browsing!

6 Advanced Tools

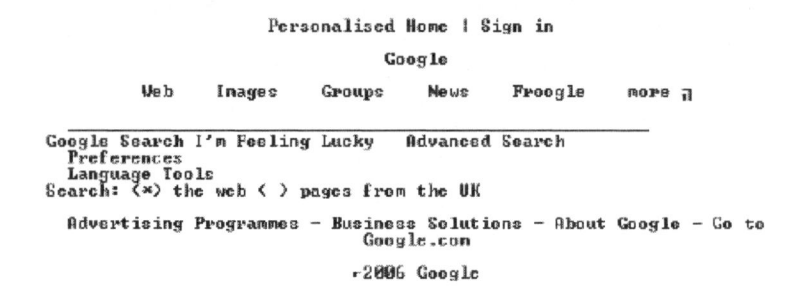

```
                    Personalised Home | Sign in
                              Google
        Web     Images    Groups    News    Froogle   more
Google Search  I'm Feeling Lucky   Advanced Search
  Preferences
  Language Tools
Search: (*) the web ( ) pages from the UK
    Advertising Programmes - Business Solutions - About Google - Go to
                              Google.com
                            ·2006 Google
```

Fig 6.1: The basic DOS-like interface of Lynx. I don't think that many people would use this for any length of time!

Accessibility

If you want to learn a lot more about this subject then I recommend that you visit the Royal National Institute for the Blind (http://www.rnib.org.uk) where there is a very well thought out section on this topic. Here you will find information on Talking Browsers and other tools used by potential visitors to your web site. Download one of these specialist browsers and use it on your web pages just to see how friendly they are. I am sure that you will find the exercise to be eye-opening!

Please don't dismiss the information as it is important. I can only advise you to do the best you can as most of us are just not skilled enough in HTML to create a perfect web site that will meet all the guidelines. Consider having a page on your web site that demonstrates your personal commitment to creating web pages that are available to everybody.

Advanced Tools **6**

Fig 6.2: The online version of the Wave Tool.

The Wave Tool can be accessed at **www.wave.webaim.org**. There is an online version and a toolbar version that is extremely difficult to install. Once you process a web site through WAVE you will get a graphical representation of:

- A number sequence of how a browser or spider will read the data on the web site.

- Information about images and the associated ALT text.

183

6 Advanced Tools

- Hidden images that a graphical web page creator has used to create that page that may well explain why an optimisation tool is giving you odd results.

Free Tools

In this section I want to introduce you to some of the free software tools that you can download from the Internet and try out for yourself. I use all the following tools on a regular basis but must confess a bias towards Web CEO.

To be honest there are not many free tools that are of very much use to the serious web page developer. The reviews that follow are my personal thoughts, so please try them out and form your own view of how useful they are. It is worth getting familiar with one or two of them as you can then cross-check results and build up your understanding of the whole process. With all these tools your personal preferences will come into play and if you don't find a tool to be intuitive to use then you should abandon it.

Free Monitor for Google

I recommend that you visit http://www.cleverstat.com and download the free Google monitor. The tool is very limited in that you only get one vital piece of information, which is ranking history. Also the free edition is limited to Google whereas the paid-for tool that starts at $99 US handles other search engines. You can download a 30-day trial of the personal or business editions and if you just want to check the ranking of your web site on a regular basis then this tool is good enough for that task.

Advanced Tools 6

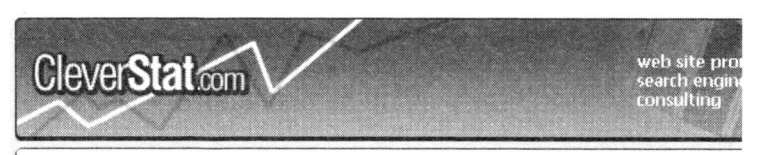

Free Monitor for Google
Free rank checking software

Free Monitor for Google is a free Web promotion software designed for search engine specialists and webmasters. With it, you can find position of your web site in Google Top for popular keywords and get more traffic from Google. Google Monitor will query Google and show you the position of your site by your target keywords and also how well your competitors are doing. It keeps statistics for several URLs and several lists of keywords. You can add notes.

Google is the most popular search engine. Monitor Google with our free software.

Fig 6.3: Free Monitor for Google. An introductory tool that leaves you desiring many more features.

Fig 6.4: The free edition in action. You just get a report that does not tell you very much!

6 Advanced Tools

Hello Engines

I include this product for completeness. The package aims to make website submission easier and has lots of screens to help generate the META tags for a web site. This isn't much use if you are using a WYSIWYG web page generator but it could, of course, help you to find any errors in that region of the web page.

The package has a 'Site Checker' button that returns a few parameters about your web site (See Figure 6.6) but offers no advice on how to fix the items that are outside its metrics. The basic version of the package comes as shareware and allows you to work with a single URL. Just a word of caution of not charging away to change your website based on the advice given by this package. I ran the 2006 edition against the same URL with the same data and the Keywords parameter is now 80.00% rather than 73.33%.

Looking on the web site of the software vendor you find very little by way of optimization advice or even to know how far short of the recommended thresholds your web site is. If you use this tool then accept the ranking advice with a high degree of caution.

Important Note

Many of the software tools will show slight discrepancies in the keyword metrics calculations. Usually they all agree on metrics that equal 100%. If you don't understand what the numbers are telling you then it best to ignore them rather than tinker blindly with your web pages in the hope that you can improve on them.

Advanced Tools 6

Fig 6.5: A screenshot of the Hello Engines control interface.

Element	Status	Rating
Description	Partly OK	86.67%
Keywords	Not OK	73.33%
Refresh	OK	100.00%
Title	OK	96.67%

Fig 6.6: The rather obscure output telling you that a couple of factors are out of tolerance.

6 Advanced Tools

Element	Status	Rating
Content	OK	100.00%
Description	Partly OK	86.67%
Keywords	Not OK	80.00%
Refresh	OK	100.00%
Title	OK	96.67%

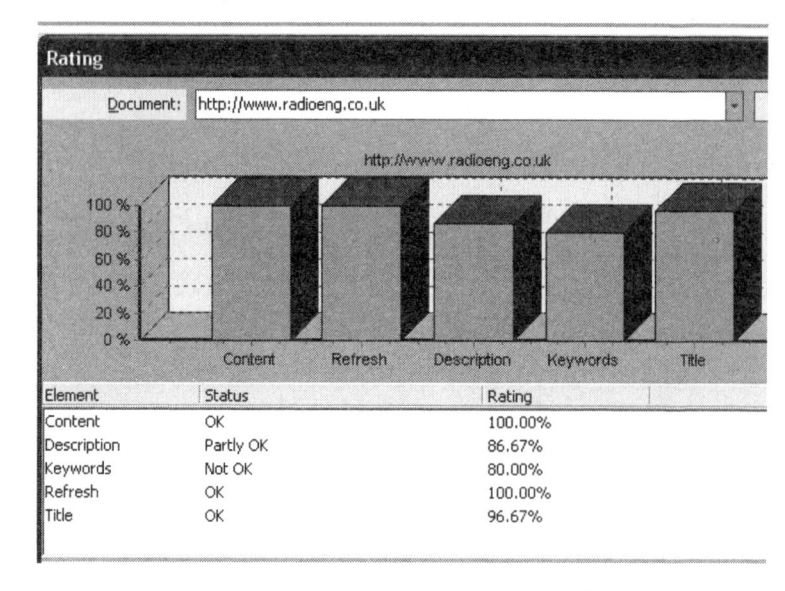

Fig 6.7: The 2006 edition has been upgraded.

Internet Business Promoter

This package has a lot of good features but in the free version you are mainly restricted as to what you can print out or save to PC. The search engine information is kept up to date and you get access to comprehensive help information. In the Free edition you do not get any program updates.

The package has two main areas covering:

- Optimization and Ranking Tools covering keywords and ranking tools. Some of the options just link into a Search Engine's site to access their tools.

Advanced Tools 6

- The spider simulation that strips away almost all the HTML to show you what the spider has seen. You can also determine the path the spider is going to take through your web page and identify the first and last sections of the web page. It is worth comparing this tool with Poodle.

- Web site submission tools split between search engines and search directories. I don't think that this tool will save you much time.

General statistics about "http://w	
Total web page size:	21,450 bytes
Visible text size:	2,714 bytes
Total size of HTML tags:	18,736 bytes
Visible text to web page size ratio:	12.65% (the more the better)
Number of images:	27

Fig 6.8: The spider simulator tells you how bloated the web page is with HTML. This page was generated by NetObjects Fusion 8 that is known to produce a lot of extraneous code.

Overall IBP gives you a different slant on one or two ranking parameters that are not supported in other packages. I do recommend that you download the free version and run it against your web site as it will provide you with some good information.

6 Advanced Tools

Optimization and ranking tools

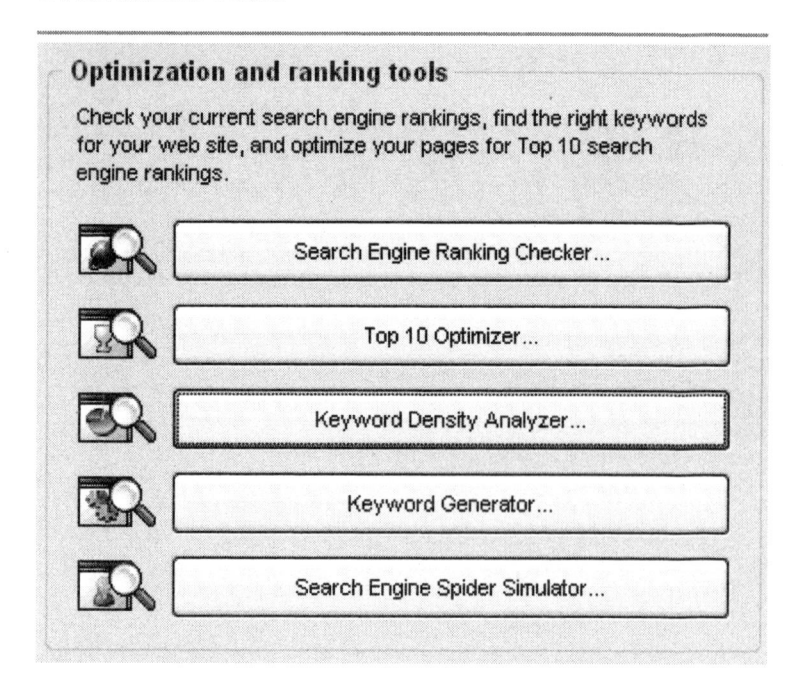

Check your current search engine rankings, find the right keywords for your web site, and optimize your pages for Top 10 search engine rankings.

- Search Engine Ranking Checker...
- Top 10 Optimizer...
- Keyword Density Analyzer...
- Keyword Generator...
- Search Engine Spider Simulator...

Fig 6.9: One half of the IBP toolbox.

The IPB optimization tools takes a slightly different approach to optimization in that it analyses the current top ten web pages in the selected search engine against your web page and then proceeds to generate a huge report on possible changes to your web page. However, in the free edition much of the advice is blocked to encourage you to buy the full version. To be honest it just generates far too much detail and you do struggle to apply the advice.

The Search Engine Spider only supports a standard browser search and the Googlebot, MSN and Yahoo spider simulators are locked off.

Advanced Tools 6

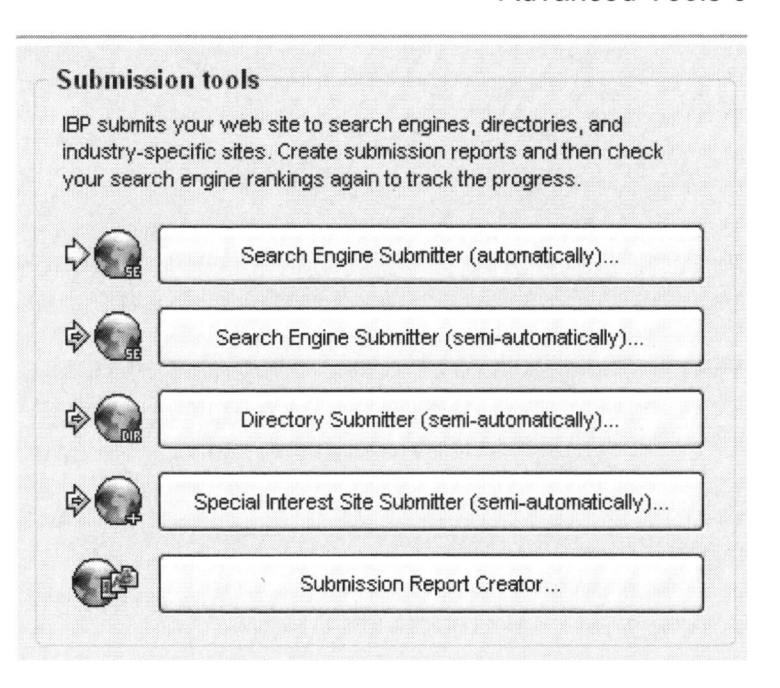

Fig 6.10: The other half of the tools.

Overall the free version is just a sampler of the full-blown product that costs just a fraction under 180 Euros for the standard version. The web site does offer a 30-day money back guarantee but I have not tried to see if this guarantee is unconditional and without any quibbles.

You can download the free trial version from this URL:

http://www.axandra.com

The HTML Validator just links to the W3C site and does not offer you any additional advice on how to correct any errors.

6 Advanced Tools

Document Title

	http://www.radioeng.co.uk/digital-radio-mondiale.html	
Keyword or key phrase	**Number of words**	**Number of characters**
digital radio mondiale	3 of 7 (42.9%)	22 of 45 (48.9%)
DRM	1 of 7 (14.3%)	3 of 45 (6.7%)

Body Text

	http://www.radioeng.co.uk/digital-radio-mondiale.html	
Keyword or key phrase	**Number of words**	**Number of characters**
digital radio mondiale	48 of 1,124 (4.3%)	352 of 6,802 (5.2%)
DRM	20 of 1,124 (1.8%)	60 of 6,802 (0.9%)

Bold Body Text

	http://www.radioeng.co.uk/digital-radio-mondiale.html	
Keyword or key phrase	**Number of words**	**Number of characters**

Fig 6.11: IBP Keyword Density analysis. The display expands if you opt to compare your page with another site.

Overall IBP brings together a comprehensive set of tools and if you like the convenience of having nearly everything you need in a single package it may just be the best tool for tracking the changes you make to your web pages.

Advanced Tools **6**

Web CEO

Web CEO also offers a free version that has many features of the full product. The software can be downloaded from this URL:

http://www.webceo.com

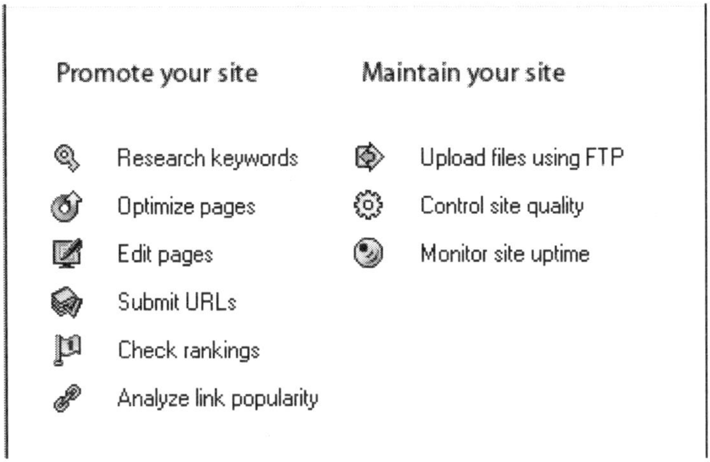

Promote your site   Maintain your site

- Research keywords   - Upload files using FTP
- Optimize pages   - Control site quality
- Edit pages   - Monitor site uptime
- Submit URLs
- Check rankings
- Analyze link popularity

Fig 6.12: Main features of the Web CEO package.

The real power of Web CEO lies in the optimization section that not only analyses your web pages but actually gives you good advice on how to change things. There is general advice and then specific advice for MSN, Google, Yahoo and Ask. I have found that the advice given is generally sound and well thought out. The optimization section provides all the standard keyword frequency, density and prominence calculations.

6 Advanced Tools

1. <HEAD> area: ⓘ

<TITLE> tag ⓘ	...
Number of Titles	1
First tag in the <HEAD> tag	Yes
Characters in Title	45
Words in Title	7
Stop words in Title	No
Keyword frequency in Title ⓘ	1
Keyword prominence in Title ⓘ	100.0%
Keyword weight in Title ⓘ	42.9%

Fig 6.13: Web CEO provides metrics on all the major parameters as well as contextual help on the more difficult topics.

Link popularity ⓘ	
Number of linking pages	50
Theme ⓘ	
Keyword presence throughout the Web site (any part of pages)	100.0%
Keyword presence throughout the Web site Titles	5.6%
Keyword presence throughout the Web site META Description	22.2%
Keyword presence throughout the Web site BODY	100.0%

Fig 6.14: Link popularity & theme provides a view on how your web site's theme is distributed across the web pages.

Advanced Tools 6

The link count is the number of pages within the search engine that are linked to this particular page on the web site. The theme is a more interesting parameter. The software has followed the links found on this page and has analysed these other pages' body text, titles and descriptions for keywords that relate back to the page being analysed. The page being analysed is from a big site with 75 pages so I am not surprised to see low scores.

Open Directory Project listing (dmoz.org)	
Web site presence	No
Keyword presence in the ODP Web site description	-
Keyword presence in the ODP category name	-
Yahoo! Directory listing	
Web site presence	No
Keyword presence in the Yahoo! Web site description	-
Keyword presence in the Yahoo! category name	-

Fig 6.15: Web CEO concentrates on the big two of the Search Engine Directory world.

Web CEO is not an intuitive package but the creators have put together a twelve-part video tutorial that takes you through all the features of the product. You really have to watch all of these or you will give up in frustration and be unable to make sense of what the product is telling you. There is also a quick-start PDF guide but this is not as helpful as seeing the actual keystroke sequences on screen. My only slight criticism is that Web CEO can focus on many rather obscure search engines which does make it slightly hard to find the major ones in the very extensive lists.

6 Advanced Tools

SEO Studio

You can download a free to use version of the product from this web site: http://www.trendmx.com. There are several restrictions in the free version but the one that will biet the hardest is that you cannot dig deeper than 30 results, which means that you are going to be working blind for a lot of the time as just won't know if the search engine is actually offering your web pages from the index.

The Standard Edition is good value at $79 and I would recommend that you purchase a copy as you can then check down to 500 results. The product isn't very clever here as it will hit the search engines at full power – I have had Google block it and send a message to my PC that they thought that I was a spammer! If you use it sensibly then you should have few problems.

The analyser gives all the information you need about all parts of the web page and more data that you could ever want. All the major parameters are readily available to you (see Figure 6.16) and you should only work with the ones that have been covered in this book rather than the more obscure ones.

To get at the very important link anchor texts that other sites are using you have to run the Links Plus+ report (See Figure 6.17). Another facility allows you to find competing pages in Google, Yahoo, MSN, Ask Jeeves, Alltheweb, Hotbot and Teoma. Helpfully it includes the same option for DMOZ and to my surprise digital radio was listed under Computers→ Multimedia->>Music. It just shows how DMOZ is slowly losing its way in terms of providing quality links! If you are having trouble finding the appropriate category in DMOZ for your web site then this package could save you a lot of time.

Advanced Tools 6

It takes a little while to get used to the software package and the Trend site does have a number of video tutorials that you can access to guide you through the process. The only thing that is missing from this package is practical web page optimization advice.

| Report | Page View | Source | Search | Keyword Suggestion |

Analyzer Report: http://www.radioeng.co.uk/digital-radio-mondi

Keyword Summary for Keyword: digital

Title(2), META Description(2), META Keywords(2), Body Text(20), Page

Title:

Title is the text placed between title tags in the HEAD section and it is u
Example: <TITLE>**title goes here**</TITLE>

| Occurrence: 2 | Density: %33 | Prominence: %71 |

Digital Radio Mondiale - **Digital** AM Radio-DRM

META Description:

Description is the text placed in the META tag in the HEAD section and is page's content.
Example: <META NAME="description" CONTENT="**description goes here**"

| Occurrence: 2 | Density: %33 | Prominence: %74 |

Digital Radio Mondiale - **digital** solution for the AM bands,

Fig 6.16: The keyword analyser is superb for a free tool. You get frequency, density & prominence in one report.

6 Advanced Tools

URL	Link Anchor Text	Page Title
www.linkopedia.com/cgi-bin/se...	Digital Radio Technology	Linkopedia: Search
www.lulu.com/digitalradio	www.radioeng.co.uk	Radio Engineering's Storefro...
iconnic.com/T57185P1-Cane-En...		Directory Listing for Cane En...
www.linkopedia.com/cgi-bin/se...	Digital Radio Technology	Linkopedia: Search
www.lulu.com/digitalradio	www.radioeng.co.uk	Radio Engineering's Storefro...
iconnic.com/T57185P1-Cane-En...		Directory Listing for Cane En...
iconnic.com/S182P1-Oxfordshir...		Directory Listing for Oxfords...
www.lulu.com/items/volume_1/...		Lulu.com - Self Publishing - F...
www.drm.org/supporters/supp...		DRM: Digital Radio Mondiale

Fig 6.17: The link anchor text information.

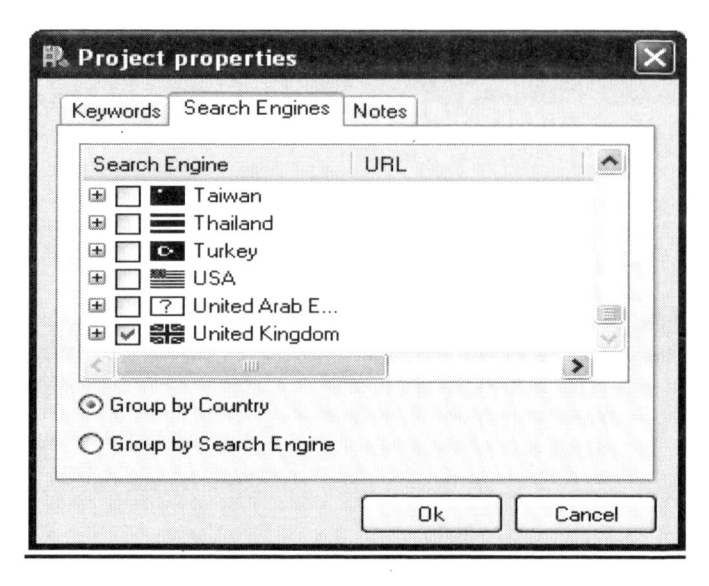

Fig 6.18: The Search Engine selection screen from the Accurate Monitor for Search Engines.

Advanced Tools **6**

Accurate Monitor For Search Engines

This is the more advanced version of the Google Free Monitor that covers more search engines and has a few more features. The screenshot in Figure 6.18 gives an idea of how extensive the search engine list is. Having selected the search engines you can then set up some additional parameters such as search depth. Here you can enter details of either the Google or Yahoo API key that you may hold. It is worth acquiring these API keys as it lets Google and Yahoo know that you will sending a large number of search requests into their systems.

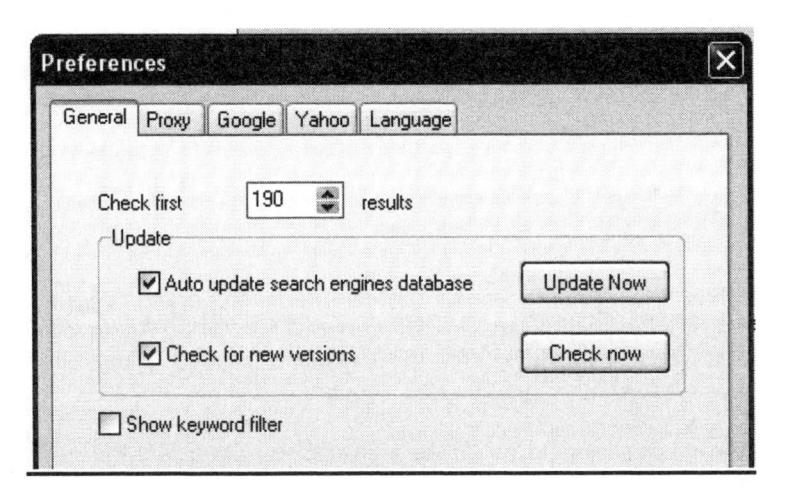

Fig 6.19: The preferences screen usefully allows you to set the search depth.

199

6 Advanced Tools

Google API

Google gets a little upset if you hit it with a huge automated set of keyword queries and fights back by blocking the search and sending a message to your PC politely asking you to stop. The Google API key allows you to make 1,000 automated queries per day. Point your browser at this URL:

http://www.googe.com/apis/

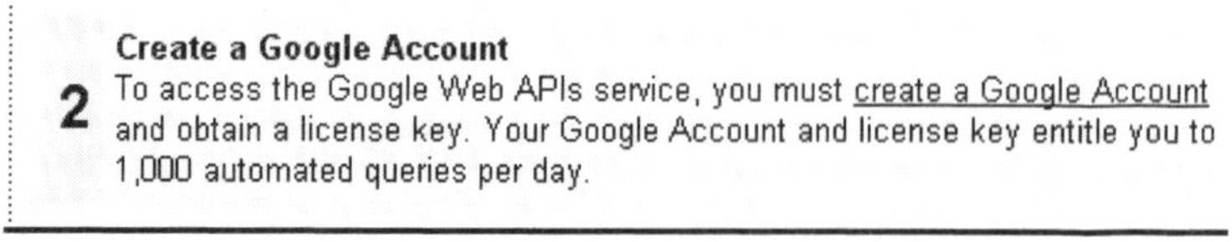

2 **Create a Google Account**
To access the Google Web APIs service, you must create a Google Account and obtain a license key. Your Google Account and license key entitle you to 1,000 automated queries per day.

Fig 6.20: Obtaining a Google API licence key is easy to do.

Yahoo API

Yahoo has a similar concept that allows developers to integrate their applications tightly in with Yahoo. The Yahoo Application ID is not a 'must have' like the Google one but it is useful to have one as part of your Yahoo account.

The quickest way to get to the registration page is via the FAQ section of the Yahoo developer network. Point your browser at this URL:

http://developer.yahoo.com/faq/

The application process is simpler than Google and you get to make up your own ID, which makes it easier to remember.

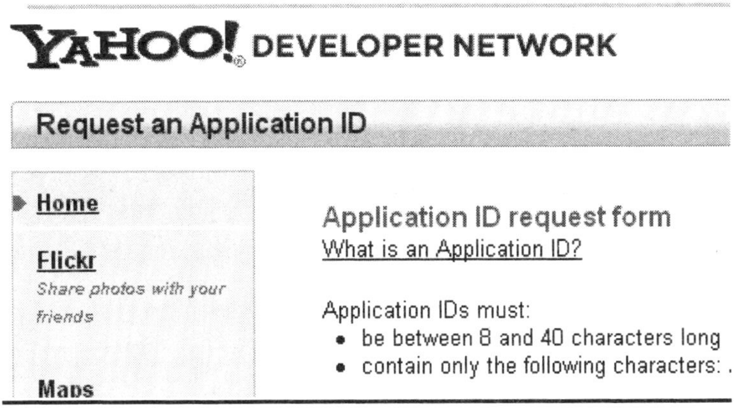

Advanced Tools **6**

YAHOO! DEVELOPER NETWORK

Request an Application ID

▶ **Home**

Flickr
Share photos with your friends

Maps

Application ID request form
What is an Application ID?

Application IDs must:
- be between 8 and 40 characters long
- contain only the following characters: .

Fig 6.21: The Yahoo API application screen.

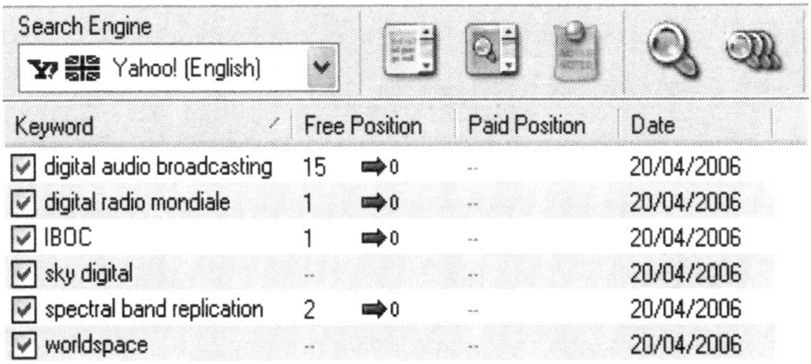

Keyword	Free Position	Paid Position	Date
digital audio broadcasting	15 ➡ 0	--	20/04/2006
digital radio mondiale	1 ➡ 0	--	20/04/2006
IBOC	1 ➡ 0	--	20/04/2006
sky digital	--	--	20/04/2006
spectral band replication	2 ➡ 0	--	20/04/2006
worldspace	--	--	20/04/2006

Search Engine: Yahoo! (English)

Fig 6.22: A nice feature of the Accurate Monitor is that is distinguishes between Free and Paid for links.

6 Advanced Tools

United Kingdom

Search engines rank summary for this country

	Lycos (English)	Excite (English)	HotBot (English)	Yahoo! (API) (English)	Abacho (English)	UK Directory (English)	Wanadoo (English)	Overture (English)	Yahoo! (English)
digital audio broadcasting	13	N/F	16	N/F	N/F	18	17	16	15
digital radio mondiale	1	N/F	2	N/F	29	11	11	1	1
IBOC	1	N/F	3	N/F	N/F	1	1	1	1
sky digital	N/F	N/F	N/F	N/F	N/F	N/F	N/F	N/F	N/F
spectral band replication	2	N/F	13	N/F	N/F	5	2	5	2
worldspace	N/F	N/F	N/F	N/F	N/F	N/F	N/F	N/F	N/F

Fig 6.23: The compact report from the Accurate Monitor.

Just How Useful are the Tools?

My experience is that no one package provided everything that I needed to manage my web sites. The packages will produce some variations on the same data as they are all estimating how the search engines actually calculate the parameters. In the table in Figure 6.24 I have compared the results from the two major packages that I use for web page analysis. There are small differences throughout but it is most marked in the body text where there is a large difference in the prominence score. This is probably to be expected as the algorithms to calculate this score have been designed by these companies themselves.

Advanced Tools 6

What is most odd is that the frequency of the keywords differs by one – I think that Web CEO is counting the keyword in a set of text links at the top of the page and as this is within the first 25 words it has boosted the keyword prominence significantly. SEO studio has determined that these are links and ignored the keywords in this area.

Parameter	Web CEO	SEO Studio
Title: keyword Frequency	1	1
Title: keyword Density	42.9%	50%
Title: Keyword Prominence	100%	100%
Desc: keyword Frequency	1	1
Desc: keyword Density	33%	50%
Desc: Keyword Prominence	100%	100%
Kwrd: keyword Frequency	1	1
Kwrd: keyword Density	50%	60%
Kwrd: Keyword Prominence	100%	100%
Body: keyword Frequency	16	15
Body: keyword Density	4.3%	5%
Body: Keyword Prominence	97.9%	61%

Fig 6.24: Comparison of SEO Studio and Web CEO.

Summary

I have covered several free packages, that can be upgraded to via the purchase of a licence key, in the preceding pages but if you need to get going quickly then get a copy of **SEO Studio** as you will then be able to quickly get that all important **ranking information**. If your web pages are already in the top ten in some search engines then you need to know that.

6 Advanced Tools

The second package that you need to acquire is **Web CEO** as this will give you good **optimization advice**. You can then master the more complicated ranking tool in Web CEO as unlike SEO Studio it keeps a history of your rankings and movements since the last scan.

Web CEO also tries to mimic the way a human uses the internet so you are much less likely to get a warning message from Google about bombarding its network with search requests. If you do trigger one of these rather ominous looking messages from Google just answer it and adjust your search parameters in the ranking tool.

Summary

The internet has many tools that claim to be able to help you manage your web pages better. At a minimum you should build up the following toolkit:

- Download and install Internet Explorer (IE), Opera & Firefox. They now work together without causing any bad effects.

- Find a compiled version of Lynx for occasional checking.

- Select one tool to check your ranking in the search engines. I recommend either Web CEO or SEO Studio.

- You need software to help optimize your web pages. I recommend either Web CEO or SEO Studio or a combination of the two.

- Get to grips with Google sitemaps if only for the analytical information that it provides.

Next Chapter

In the next chapter I cover the world of the search engine robots and how you can control them.

7. Controlling the Robots

We have touched on the major ways of controlling what the search engines access on your web site. There are two ways to influence all search engines and this is by using META tags or the robots.txt file. You can also influence Google by using the Google Sitemaps facility but all three will need to be in harmony. If you have created an additional site map navigation page then you need to make sure that it is also in harmony with all the others. Search engines love links and will find them even when you don't want them to!

Important Notes

I use the word 'influence' as there is nothing you can do to prevent a URL being indexed – you can only prevent the content from being indexed.

Just to be clear the robots.txt file takes precedence over the META robots tag. The logic behind this is that the META information can only be read by the robot actually reading the contents of the web page. It can only do this if the robots.txt file allows it to access the information.

Most web site hosting companies allow the use of the robots.txt file as having purchased web space from a company you should have FTP access to the root (top) level of the domain where the robots.txt file must live. META tags can be used instead of this option. Also note that the robots.txt file is respected by way of a gentleman's agreement if you like. A search engine robot or other automated piece of software can ignore the file.

Controlling the Robots 7

The robots.txt file has no real lockout capability. It is only a text file after all expressing your wishes and not an operating system file like the .htaccess that the server will enforce.

robots.txt

One of the first things that any of these robots do is to look for a file called robots.txt in the highest level directory (usually called the root directory of the www side of the site.) The 'www' side of the site is different to where you upload the web pages to. You can create this file with Notepad – do not use WordPad or any other editor that uses rich text as it will add in too many other characters. The database of robots lists nearly 300 robots but luckily you will not be interested in that many.

Search Engine	Name
Google	Googlebot
MSN	MSNbot
Yahoo	Slurp**
Alexa	Alexa (IA Archiver)
Inktomi	Slurp**
Looksmart	WISENutBot
Ask	AskJeeves

** Same robot.

Fig 7.1: Table of the major robots. Some robots identify themselves by name, others by IP.

This file tells the robot how it can crawl through your site. This file can be used to exclude some or all of your web site from named robots or all robots. You need to get it right!

7 Controlling the Robots

The simplest file shown in Figure 7.2 is almost empty and allows all robots access to every part of your site. Note that the focus is on prevention (disallow) rather than access. A very similar file is shown in Figure 7.3. Here you have stopped all the robots (denoted by the wildcard character '*') searching any part of your site (denoted by the '/' character than equates to the root directory level of the site).

You might want to use this technique if you have a members-only or closed users' group type of site that you publicise off-line. The files provide a certain level of invisibility and are not foolproof.

```
User-agent: *
Disallow:
```

Fig 7.2: This simple file lets all the robots look at everything on the site. There are no restrictions.

```
User-agent: *
Disallow: /
```

Fig 7.3: This file stops all the robots looking at any part of your site.

A much more complex robots.txt file is shown in Figure 7.4. This one is aimed at stopping Google from crawling into the e-commerce and other private areas on one of my web sites. The other robots (designated by '*') are allowed into more directories as they seem to make more intelligent decisions.

Controlling the Robots 7

Even then I wasn't 100% sure that Google was really obeying the full instructions as it rather doggedly held on to the entries it had found in previous visits to the web site. Overall it will take you several months to 'tame' the Googlebot and you will have to use all the techniques at your disposal to achieve your objectives.

```
User-agent: Googlebot

Disallow: /dl82adrm/
Disallow: /nladamint/
Disallow: /catalogue/
Disallow: /newsletters/PDF/
User-agent: *

Disallow: /dl82adrm/
Disallow: /nladamint/
Disallow:
```

Fig 7.4: Here is a complicated file that stops Google digging into various areas of a web site.

META Tags

The other way to direct the robots is via HTML coding. This may be your only option sometimes, if the web site administrator prevents you from accessing the root directory. Most commercial hosting companies allow you access to this area via FTP so you are unlikely to have any problems nowadays.

7 Controlling the Robots

Where to put the Robots META tag

Like any META tag it should be placed in the HEAD section of an HTML page:

```
<html>
<head>
<meta name="robots" content="noindex, nofollow">
<meta name="description" content="This page ....">
<title>...</title>
</head>
<body>
```

What to put into the Robots META tag

The content of the Robots META tag contains directives separated by commas. The currently defined directives are [NO]INDEX and [NO]FOLLOW.

The INDEX directive specifies if an indexing robot should index the page. The FOLLOW directive specifies if a robot is to follow links on the page.

The defaults are INDEX and FOLLOW. The values ALL and NONE set all directives on or off: ALL=INDEX, FOLLOW and NONE=NOINDEX, NOFOLLOW

There is another META tag that tells the robot to include or exclude you from the search engine's cache. This is the [NO]ARCHIVE tag that operates just like the other operators. The cache comes into its own if your web site is off line – the search engine will serve up pages from its cache until your site comes back on line.

```
<html>
<head>
<meta name="googlebot" content="noarchive">
<meta name="description" content="This page is not be cached ....">
<title>...</title>
</head>
<body>
```

If you use a web page creation tool check what it is putting into these META tags as the defaults may not be want you want.

Google Sitemaps

Google is always inventing new ways to improve its index. The launch of Google Sitemaps caused a huge stir and was promoted by many people as a way to shoot up the rankings. There is no doubt that it helps your listing as Google takes notice of the information that you put in there.

The name actually tells you the purpose and that is to make sure that the Google robot finds all the links, images and web pages that you want it to. You can also tell it how often you refresh your pages. Google does moves information around so I have found that the best way to get to any of their services is to start here at the webmaster's area:

http://www.google.com/webmasters

From there you should find a link to the sitemaps page. The first thing that you will notice is that the whole process seems rather complicated as Google provides an extensive specification for you to follow.

7 Controlling the Robots

Google does provide a sitemap generator that is unfortunately written in one of the least common server scripting languages called Python. Some hosting companies allow it and some do not.

General server information:

Operating system	Linux
Service Status	Click to View
Kernel version	2.4.21-40.ELsmp
Machine Type	i686
Apache version	1.3.34 (Unix)
PERL version	5.8.7
Path to PERL	/usr/bin/perl
Path to sendmail	/usr/sbin/sendmail
Installed Perl Modules	Click to View
PHP version	4.4.2
MySQL version	4.1.18-standard
cPanel Build	10.8.1-STABLE 114
Theme	cPanel X v2.5.0
Documentation	Click to View

Fig 7.5: This host does not support Python. This information was extracted from the cPanel control.

Controlling the Robots 7

Services	
Apache ASP support	✓
SSI support	✓
PHP support	✓
CGI support	✓
mod_perl support	✓
mod_python support	✓

Fig 7.6: This hosting company supports python.

Even if you can run a python script on your server the hosting company may still not allow you to connect to the server at the level that Google suggests.

Important Note

Connecting to a web server can happen at several levels. Web hosting companies like customers to connect via established and safe methods such as HTTP and FTP. Google sitemaps needs access via SSH, which is the short name for a Secure Shell (SSH). It is a program to log into another computer over a network, to execute commands in a remote machine, and to move files from one machine to another. It provides strong authentication and secure communications over unsecured channels. If all this makes no sense to you then my recommendation is to keep away from it.

7 Controlling the Robots

Other developers have taken the idea on board and I now use a product called GSiteCrawler that runs under Windows on my PC. This is much more convenient than trying to work in the unfamiliar world of Linux.

GSiteCrawler

First of all you will have to download the product from the author's website (http://johannesmueller.com/gs) and install it on your PC – this is all very straightforward and you should not have any problems. Regular updates are usually issued every two or three months.

Project	Settings	Filter	URL list

Project name:

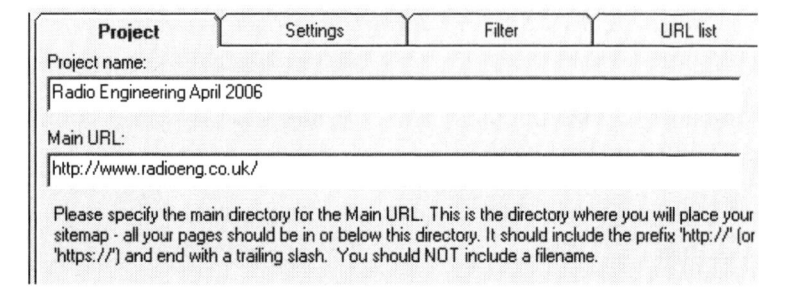

Radio Engineering April 2006

Main URL:

http://www.radioeng.co.uk/

Please specify the main directory for the Main URL. This is the directory where you will place your sitemap - all your pages should be in or below this directory. It should include the prefix 'http://' (or 'https://') and end with a trailing slash. You should NOT include a filename.

Fig 7.7: The initial project set-up screen for GSiteCrawler.

You need to take the steps slowly otherwise you will end up with a mangled sitemap file. First of all set up the project name and the main URL as shown in Figure 7.7 and then add it to the list of projects.

The next tab is for settings and to keep things simple you can just tick the box if you are using a Linux server and ignore the FTP and Automation tabs.

Controlling the Robots 7

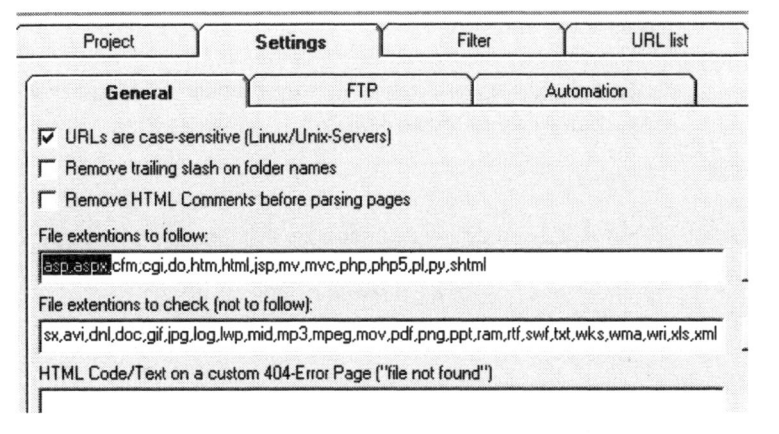

Fig 7.8: The configuration possibilities are extensive.

The defaults file extensions to follow are 'htm' and 'html'. Clicking the default buttons will add in many more files and you can edit this list to your particular requirements. If you just want to evaluate the product's features then just leave the basic HTML file options.

I would advise you to ignore the Filter Tab until you are more familiar with the project.

Moving on to the URL tab you are presented with a table that will be populated when the crawler finishes checking your site.

- Manual

    When this is checked, you are manually confirming the URL. These URLs are not deleted when you click on the 'Delete all non-manual URLs' button. Usually, you would use this to confirm the URL as being correct.

7 Controlling the Robots

- Include

    URLs which have 'Include' checked will be included in the generated sitemap XML file.

- Priority

    This is the priority as passed to the Google Sitemap. It is a relative priority from 0.0 to 1.0. Higher priority values do not mean a higher search ranking.

- Frequency

    Here you can specify how often Google 'should' look at this URL. It is not a command, but rather a hint. The days specified here are translated to Google's listing: 0=always, 1-6=daily, 7-29=weekly, 30-299=monthly, 300-998=yearly, 999=never.

- Crawl

    When this is checked, the crawler will also crawl from this URL the next time it is started.

You can bring up the screen that shows that crawler's progress to make sure that it is actually doing something. The software can be stubborn and not start sometimes but it will with a bit of encouragement. Once you get the messages that the 'Crawlers are now Empty' you can refresh the table and the blank screen shown in Figure 7.9 gets filled with data as shown in Figure 7.10.You must edit this data as it will be full of links that you don't want Google to index.

It is all a bit laborious but once you master the basic steps the process becomes logical and you will find it very easy to generate a Sitemaps XML file.

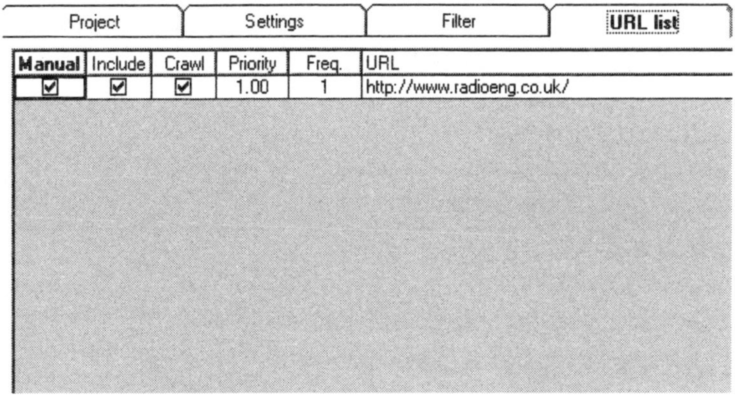

Controlling the Robots 7

Fig 7.9: The URL list starts with a single entry.

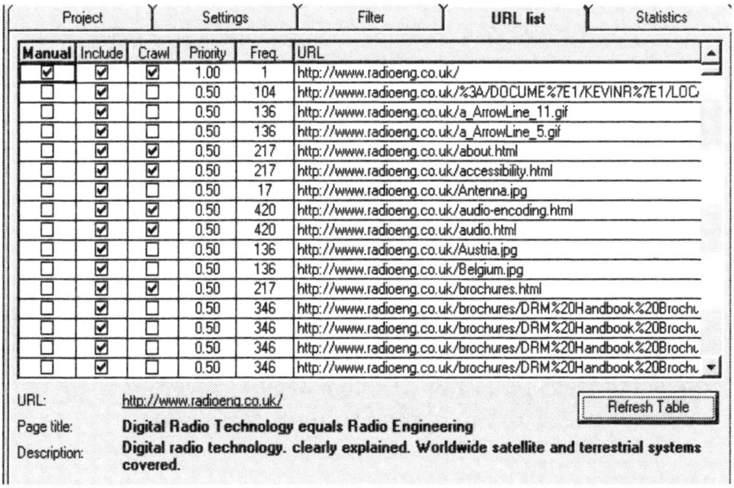

Fig 7.10: The crawl process will produce a huge list of potential files.

217

7 Controlling the Robots

In this example the crawler found about 550 URLs and in the end I deleted some 500 of them to create a compact list. You edit the list via a set of buttons at the bottom of the window.

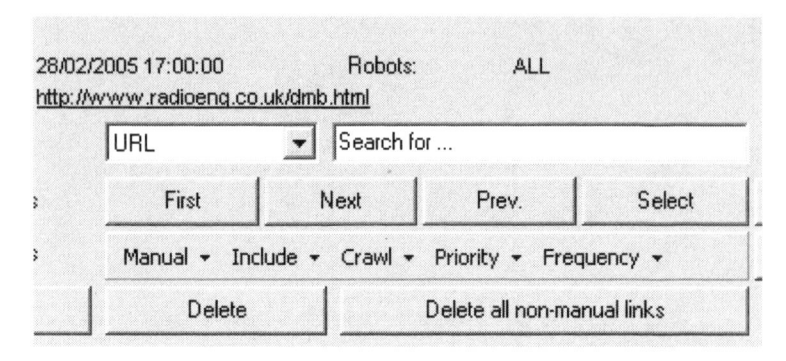

Fig 7.11: The control panel lets you delete any URLs that you do not want included in the site map.

Fig 7.12: The 'generate' process should produce a set of files in the named project directory.

The final step is to generate the actual XML-based file map to load up onto web server via your FTP client.

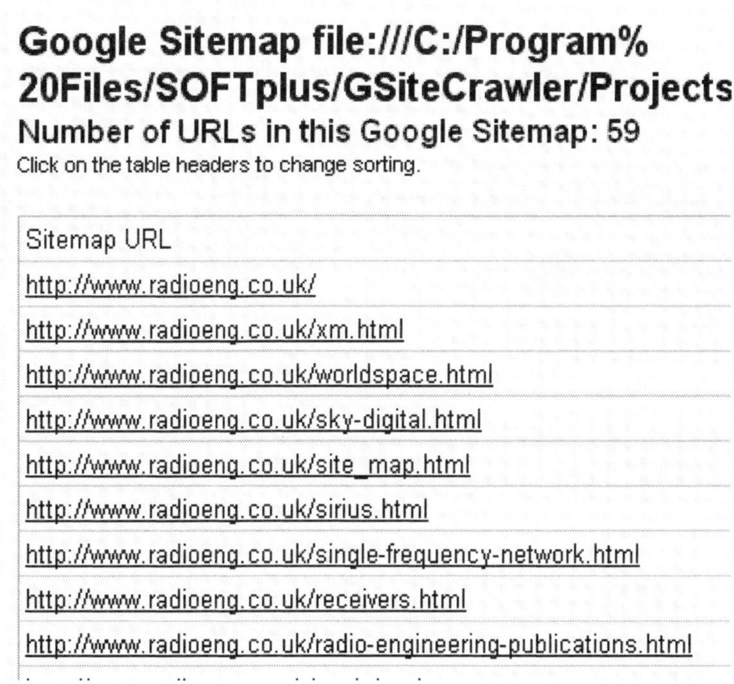

Google Sitemap file:///C:/Program%20Files/SOFTplus/GSiteCrawler/Projects
Number of URLs in this Google Sitemap: 59
Click on the table headers to change sorting.

Sitemap URL
http://www.radioeng.co.uk/
http://www.radioeng.co.uk/xm.html
http://www.radioeng.co.uk/worldspace.html
http://www.radioeng.co.uk/sky-digital.html
http://www.radioeng.co.uk/site_map.html
http://www.radioeng.co.uk/sirius.html
http://www.radioeng.co.uk/single-frequency-network.html
http://www.radioeng.co.uk/receivers.html
http://www.radioeng.co.uk/radio-engineering-publications.html

Fig 7.13: You can check the Sitemap file in a browser.

Google Sitemaps Interface

To gain access to the wealth of information that Google provides via the Sitemaps facility you need to create an account. If you obtained an API key from Google or have registered for any other service then that single user ID & password should work with Google Sitemaps.

7 Controlling the Robots

There is a verification process via e-mail but once this is done you can register your first sitemap with Google. Just look for the 'Add' tab near to the Google logo and provide the URL of the web site that you want to add to the list. There is one final step where Google requests that you place a special file in the root area of your web server. The file is empty but it proves to Google that you are actually the owner of the web site.

| Site Overview | Add |

Site Overview
Click a site to view information about it and its related Sitemaps.

Download as .csv file
More downloads

View: [All sites ▼] [OK]   View stats for: [   ]

Site ▼
☐ See stats for: http://www.digital-radio-mondiale-consultancy.co.uk/
☐ See stats for: http://www.kpriservices.co.uk/
☐ See stats for: http://www.masterwebbiz.com/
☐ See stats for: http://www.micro-business-index.com/
☐ See stats for: http://www.radioeng.co.uk/

[Delete Selected]

Fig 7.14: One of the Google sitemaps screens where you see an overview of all your sites.

Controlling the Robots 7

Sitemap	Site Verified?
1	✓
1	✓
1	✓
1 ERRORS 1	✓
Add a Sitemap	Verify
1	✓

Fig 7.15: The second half of the overview screen will tell you if you have any errors or if you are monitoring a web site without a sitemap.

Once you have sent the file to your web site via FTP and confirmed it, Google will access this file immediately and will then add your sitemap to their list to be checked and even this will happen in a day or so.

Figure 7.16 shows some of the really valuable information that Google Sitemaps provide for you. This shows just a part of a much longer list and gives details of when Google provided one of the web pages in response to a search.

Other information includes whether there are any problems with any part of the web site, the status of the robots.txt file and much more. There is extensive help within the section of Google to help you understand and eliminate any errors. I do recommend that you sign up and try it out.

7 Controlling the Robots

Top searches

Download as .csv file

Top search queries	Average top position
1. "t dmb"	14
2. hisrory	3
3. drm2	10
4. hisrory channel	2
5. parametric stereo	26
6. the human ear	7
7. iboc	31
8. orthogonal frequency division multiplexing	28
9. drm simulcast	34
10. why use 9 khz	9
11. drm radio	104
12. frequency division multiplexing	131

Fig 7.16: More valuable information about the searches that are hitting your web pages.

ALEXA Toolbar

Alexa has set itself up as the archivist of the internet and gathers selective information about web sites. Alexa has a toolbar that can be added to your web browser. The toolbar can be downloaded from http://www.alexa.com and is usually a trouble free installation. I always take the time to register my web sites with Alexa so that the information displayed looks professional. Alexa monitors traffic to your web site and provides valuable information about the popularity of your web site.

Controlling the Robots 7

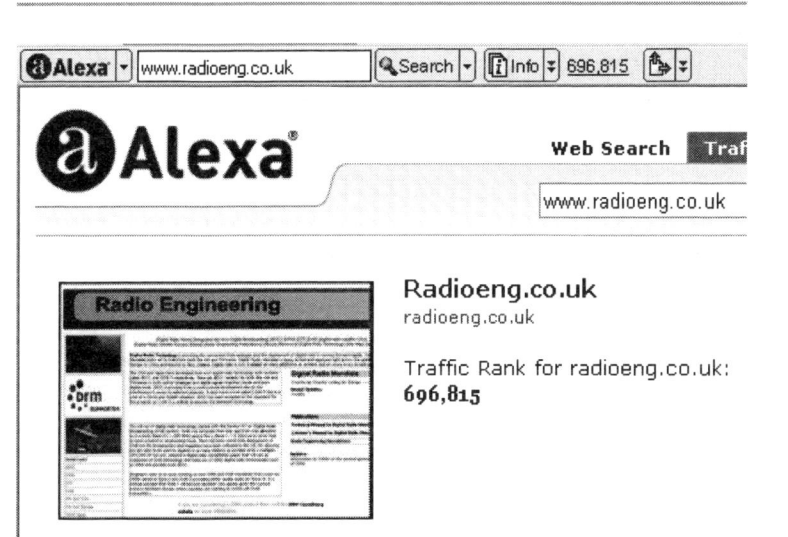

Fig 7.17: A typical Alexa entry showing a thumbnail of the web site and some traffic details.

Site Stats for radioeng.co.uk:

- **Traffic Rank for radioeng.co.uk:** 696,815 (⬇404,595)
- **Speed:** Very Fast (88% of sites are slower), Avg Load Time: .7 Seconds
- **Other sites that link to this site:** No Data
- **Online Since:** 15-Nov-2004

Fig 7.18: Alexa showing a bad month for this web site.

7 Controlling the Robots

Alexa has extensive online help about the statistics that it gathers. The data within Alexa is just a guide as to how many people are visiting your site relative to other sites and is gathered from other Alexa users.

Summary

The internet has many tools that claim to be able to help you manage your web pages better. At a minimum you should build up the following toolkit:

- Download and install Internet Explorer (IE), Opera & Firefox. They now work together without causing any bad effects.

- Find a compiled version of Lynx for occasional checking.

- Select one tool to check you ranking in the search engines. I recommend either Web CEO or SEO Studio.

- You need software to help optimize your web pages. I recommend either Web CEO or SEO Studio or a combination of the two.

- Get to grips with Google sitemaps if only for the analytical information that it provides.

Controlling the Robots 7

Creating high-ranking web sites is sometimes an art and at other times it demands a methodical and more technical approach.

The best thoughts that I can leave you with are these. Whatever you have to deal with you must not get despondent and give up. The internet gets more crowded every day and this will bring new challenges to every web site owner. Keep up to date with developments and make a point of monitoring your web pages on a regular basis. Finally, keep adding new content to your web site to keep the search engine robots happy!

Glossary

A

Accessibility is about your web site being accessible to the whole population including those with physical impairments.

Acronym is a word formed from the initial letters of other words. Try not to use them as your main keywords. There is also a HTML tag of the same name.

Adwords is Google's Pay per Click or Sponsored Search results system.

ALT is an option within the <IMG> HTML tag that is used to provide a textual description of the associated image. This text can contain keywords but it should really be used to describe the image for accessibility reasons.

Anchor is a HTML tag that allows you to create links within or between web pages.

The HTML code to link between web pages has the general form of: <A HREF=http://www.domain.com/>anchor text</a>. If the 'anchor text portion contains a keyword or two then this scores a plus point with the search engines.

B

Backlink is another name for an Inbound Link.

Glossary

Black Hat Techniques are unprofessional tricks used to scam the search engines into ranking web pages higher that they would normally be.

Body is the main part of a web page that is found between the <BODY> and </BODY> HTML tags.

Breadcrumbs is a site navigation technique that creates a set of links from the start page to the current page.

Broken Link is a link to a web page or web site that does not work.

C

Cache is where the search engines store copies of your web pages so that they can still be fed to customers even if the actual web page is temporarily unavailable.

Click Through or Clickthrough is where you click on a link in a search engine's results page to be taken to a web page stored in the search engine's index.

Click Through Rate (CTR) is a measurement of how often a web page is selected when offered as part of a search engine results page.

Cross links is where the owner of several domains links all the sites together even though the web pages have little in common with each other. Problems can arise if this is overused.

Glossary

CSS stands for Cascading Style Sheets and is a companion of HTML. CSS is used to separate style from the content and structure provided by HTML.

D

Deep Links or **Deep Pages** are found well down in a web site's directory structure and may be ignored by the search engine robots.

DHTML stands for Dynamic HTML and combines HTML, CSS and scripting together. HTML defines the structure, CSS how those elements are rendered and scripting allows the elements to be changed in response to a user's input.

Domain is the textual form of the numeric (actual) address of a web site. Domain Name Servers translate between the two forms.

Doorway Page is a page specifically designed to be ranked highly by a particular search engine. Different doorway pages are offered to different search engines and actual visitors. This is a Black Hat Technique.

Dynamic Pages are web pages generated in response to a user's input.

E

Entry Point is a web page where a user enters your web site.

Glossary

External Link same as an Outbound Link.

F

File Transfer Protocol or FTP is used to move files between computers.

Frames are used to display several independent web pages on a single screen or window.

Frameset is a HTML tag that will specify the attributes of the multi-page window and also contain <FRAME> tags that specify the source web-page and its visual characteristics.

G

Gateway Page is the same as a Doorway Page.

H

Head is the HTML tag that contains the document information such as <TITLE> and the <META> tags.

Headings H1 to H6 where H1 is the major heading tag, H2 a sub-heading and H3 is a subtopic within that sub-section.

HTML is a mark-up language used to define web page content and structure.

Glossary

HTTP stands for the Hyper Text Transfer Protocol that specifies how web pages are transferred between a web host and a user's PC.

I

Image Map is a large graphic with clickable hot-spots that serve as links to other web pages.

Inbound link is a one-way link from an external web page to your web page.

K

Keyphrase is a group of keywords.

Keyword is a word or search term that web users enter into a search query box to create a search engine results page that will have 10 web pages ranked in order of relevance to the query.

Keyword Effectiveness Index is a way of ranking the keywords in terms of popularity and competition. A high KEI means that there are many searches but few web pages having that keyword in them.

Keyword Density is the ratio of the Keyword Frequency to the total number of words found in a particular area of a web page.

Keyword Frequency is how often a Keyword appears on a particular area of a page.

Glossary

Keyword Prominence is how close a Keyword is to the start of a particular area of a page.

Keyword Proximity is how close individual words in a keyword phrase are to each other.

Keyword Stuffing is adding unnecessary keywords to an area of a page to influence any of the above parameters.

Keyword Weight is the same as Keyword Density.

Keywords is a HTML <META> tag found in the <HEAD> region of the document.

L

Landing Page is the same as an Entry Point.

Link Popularity is a measure of how many qualified inbound links are coming into your web site.

M

META is a set of HTML tags that carry information about the web page or document.

N

Navigation is about the features offered to users to help them move around a web site.

Glossary

O

Off The Page Optimization is about those factors that are on web pages external to a web site that are judged by search engines to be important in ranking a web page.

Optimization is about making changes to a web page to improve its ranking in a search engine.

On the Page Optimization are factors on a web page such as content, headings, etc. that are evaluated by a search engine.

Organic Results are not sponsored or paid-for search results.

Outbound Link is a link from one of your web pages to another web site.

P

Page Rank is a value assigned to a web page within a search engine.

PageRank is Google's technology used to calculate their version of Page Rank

Pay-Per-Click is another name for sponsored results.

PERL, PHP, PYTHON are scripting languages found on web hosts.

Glossary

Q

Query is a keyword or group of keywords with or without additional qualification that is entered into a search box to initiate a retrieval of information from a search engine's index.

R

Reciprocal Links is where inbound and outbound links are exchanged between two web sites.

Relevancy is how closely a result matches the query entered into a search engine. It is usually scored between 0 and 1.

Robot is a piece of software that extracts and analyses the content of a web site. The robot can be controlled by entries in the robots.txt file and or a META tag.

S

Sandbox is a safe test area away from the main system.

Script is a set of instructions written in a programming language that carries out certain operations.

SERP stands for a Search Engine Results Page, which is a formatted list of web pages and documents that match the search query.

Site Map is a HTML page with links to all important web pages and documents contained within a web site. This is not the same as a Google Sitemap.

Glossary

Stem is a part of a word to which inflections are added. For example 'install' can expand to 'installation' and 'installing'.

T

Theme is central subject that joins all the elements of your web site together.

Topic is a subject that is related to your theme or central subject matter.

U

URL stands for Uniform Resource Locator and nowadays it means an individual web page.

W

Web Log is an online diary.

X

XHTML is a web language half way between HTML and XML and is an XML compliant version of HTML

XML stands for eXtensible Markup Language and is a web language that is adaptable to almost any need.

Appendix 1

The next few pages show the completed keyword matrix for the Cead Books web site. The matrix is large so it is split across several pages.

TABLE 4			
Code	**Level**	**Keyword (s)**	**Comments**
A	Topic	Mysteries	Primary single keyword
B	Topic	Civilizations	Primary single keyword
A1	Level 2	Ancient Mysteries	Secondary keyword or 2 keyword phrase
A2	Level 2	Ancient Civilizations	Secondary keyword or 2 keyword phrase
B1	Level 2	Lost Civilisations	Secondary keyword or 2 keyword phrase
B2	Level 2	Prehistory	Secondary keyword or 2 keyword phrase

Fig AP1.1: The high level part of the keyword matrix.

Appendix 1

A1a	Level 3	Mysteries Ancient Egypt	Keyword phrases of 2 to 3 words
A1b	Level 3	Mysteries Ancient World	Keyword phrases of 2 to 3 words
A2a	Level 3	Ancient India	Keyword phrases of 2 to 3 words
A2b	Level 3	Ancient History	Keyword phrases of 2 to 3 words
B1a	Level 3	Lost City Atlantis	Keyword phrases of 2 to 3 words
B1b	Level 3	Lost Empire Atlantis	Keyword phrases of 2 to 3 words
B2a	Level 3	Prehistory Timeline	Keyword phrases of 2 to 3 words
B2b	Level 3	Antiquity prehistory	Keyword phrases of 2 to 3 words

Fig AP1.2: The second part of the keyword matrix that shows the next level down.

Appendix 1

B1a1	Level 4	Lost Continent Mu Lemuria	Keyword phrases of 2 to 4 words
A1b2	Level 4		Keyword phrases of 2 to 4 words
A2a1	Level 4	Ancient History Mysteries	Keyword phrases of 2 to 4 words
A2a2	Level 4		Keyword phrases of 2 to 4 words
A2b1	Level 4		Keyword phrases of 2 to 4 words
A2b2	Level 4		Keyword phrases of 2 to 4 words

Fig AP1.3: The final level where I ran out of useful three or four word phrases.

Ancient Mysteries History Civilisations
Books on the **ancient mysteries** of lost civilisations
www.cead-books.co.uk   Cached page

Ancient Mysteries
Comparisons between the civilizations of **Ancient** E
edgarcayce.org/am   Cached page   17/05/2006

Fig AP1.4: This web site is still at the number one position in MSN.

Appendix 1

Keyword Phrases	Best Position	Notes
Ancient Mysteries	MSN - 1 Yahoo (UK) - 12 Altavista (UK) - 14 Overture (UK) - 14 Looksmart - 14	
Ancient Mysteries Egypt	MSN - 4 Yahoo - 7 Overture (UK) - 9 UKplus - 9 Looksmart - 9 Altavista(UK) - 11	Webcrawler - 33 Yahoo -20
Lost Civilisations	MSN - 6 Yahoo (UK) - 8 Looksmart - 14 Overture(UK) - 13 Altavista(UK) - 22 Dogpile - 4	AlltheWeb - 15 Altavista - 17 Yahoo - 13 Yahoo(AUS) - 27 FindiT - 15 Webcrawler - 34
Ancient Mysteries Egypt	MSN - 4 Yahoo(UK) - 7 Looksmart - 9 Overture - 9 UKPlus - 9	
Ancient Civilisations	Altavista - 19 Looksmart -18 MSN - 18 Overture - 18 Yahoo - 16	
New Chronology	0	
Lost City Atlantis	0	
Ancient India	MSN - 46	
Lost continent Mu Lemuria	Yahoo - 2 Altavista - 2	Altavista - 29 Yahoo(AUS) - 42

Appendix 1

	MSN - 3 UKPlus - 4 Overture - 4 Looksmart - 4 Lycos - 4 Google - 26 AOL - 26	Yahoo - 28 Alltheweb - 29
Lost Empire Atlantis	MSN - 35	
Prehistory Timeline	0	
Mysteries Ancient World	MSN - 6 Looksmart - 41 Overture - 37	

Fig AP1.5: Ranking changes following the first iteration of changes. A vast improvement on the original web site.

Index

Accessibility 182
Alexa search engine 129
Alexa Toolbar 222
ALT image tag 36
Altavista search engine 93
ASK search engine 39, 123, 145, 175
Breadcrumbs trail 51
Digitalpoint keyword tool 74
DMOZ 11, 13, 15, 31, 98, 111, 119
File extensions 52
File names 52
Four-tier structure 61
FRAMESET tag 38
Google AdSense 155
Google AdWords 144
Google API 200
Google PageRank 27
Google Sandbox 22
Google search engine 99, 123, 177
Google Sitemaps 211
Google spider emulator 124
Google Toolbar 28
Google URL Submission 34
header tag 44
HREF type links 38
HTML validation 44

Index

HTTP 404 error	132, 139, 142
HTTP 500 error	143
Inktomi search engine	40, 129
Keyword Density	87
Keyword Effectiveness Index	82
Keyword Frequency	164
Keyword Prominence	166
Keyword stuffing	87
Keyword Weight	164
Keywords	62
link command	117
Meta Tags	89
Misspellings	83
MSN Business Directory	16
MSN search engine	106, 172
Navigation menus	51
Niche Search Engines	4
NOFRAMES tag	38
Overture	74, 77
PageRank	23, 62, 88
Pay Per Click	17, 144
PayPal	115
Poodle spider emulator	125
robots.txt file	130
Search Behaviour	24
Search Engine Categories	3
Search Engine Directories	12
Search Engine Market Share	7
Search Engine Relationships	9

Index

site command 122
Site map 53, 89
SRC type link 38
Web Behaviour 23
Web Page Description 93, 163
Web page theme 55, 96
Web Page Titles 93, 162
Web site theme 54
Wordtracker 74
Yahoo API 200
Yahoo Directory 16
Yahoo search engine 109, 177